The Prospective Spouse Checklist

The Prospective Spouse Checklist

Evaluating Your Potential Partner

By

Isabelle Fox, Ph.D.
and Robert M. Fox, J.D.

New Horizon Press
Far Hills, NJ

646.77
704

Fox, Isabelle and Fox, Robert M.
The Prospective Spouse Checklist: Evaluating Your Potential Partner
Cover design: Robert Aulicino
Interior design: Susan Sanderson

Library of Congress Control Number: 2011923245

ISBN-13: 978-0-88282-375-1
New Horizon Press

Manufactured in the U.S.A.

15   14   13   12   11   1   2   3   4   5

Authors' Note

This book is based on the authors' research, personal experiences and clients' real life experiences. In order to protect privacy, names have been changed and identifying characteristics have been altered except for contributing experts.

For purposes of simplifying usage, the pronouns he/she and him/her are sometimes used interchangeably. The information contained herein is not meant to be a substitute for professional evaluation and therapy with mental health professionals.

dedication

Our book is dedicated to our seven grandchildren:
Alexander, Laura, Ben, Anna, Amanda, Jeffrey and Sophie

Contents

Preface   ix

chapter one   Defining Love   1

chapter two   Examining a Relationship   13
Without Structured Evaluation

chapter three   Understanding the Prospective   21
Spouse Checklist and Its Function

chapter four   Applying the Checklist to a Relationship   127

chapter five   Using Dating, Courtship and   149
Engagement as Learning Periods

chapter six   Searching for a Spouse   163

chapter seven   Overcoming the Challenges   181
of Remarriage

Conclusion   201
Afterword   203
Acknowledgements   205
Notes   207
Index   213
Appendix: The Prospective Spouse Checklist   219

Preface

The selection of a spouse and the decision to marry are two of life's most crucial decisions. Be aware the result of your choice will have ongoing reverberations. It may determine the amount of stress you feel in the years to come, how long you live, your sense of security and satisfaction and whether you will suffer years of boredom, conflict and misery or years of bliss, happiness and growth. Author David McCullough writes in his biography *John Adams* about the entire married life of John and Abigail Adams: fifty-four years, until the death of Abigail at age seventy-three. Concerning Adams' marriage to Abigail Smith, McCullough comments: "It was the most important decision of his life." We agree! The wise and careful selection of a mate is invaluable. McCullough shows how expertly Abigail continually fulfilled her four essential spouse roles (discussed in chapter 3), in particular the wisdom and good judgment in her advice to our second president.[1] It also confirms another key concept: a wise marital decision can bring many decades of deep satisfaction to a married couple.

Many people are concerned about the dangerous deterioration of perhaps our most important institution: marriage—and the family it is expected to create, protect and nurture. According to the National Kids Count Program, 34 percent of all United States children now live in single-parent homes. Some states have much higher percentages; the figure is 48 percent in Mississippi.[2] According to the United States Department of Health and Human Services 2010 report titled "Births: Final Data for 2008," 40.6 percent of all United States births are to unmarried women.[3] Nuclear families (mom, dad and children together) are on the decline. The institution of marriage is under quiet, but relentless, attack. According to marriage authority and author John Gottman, in his book *The Seven Principles for Making Marriage Work,* divorce now destroys 67 percent of all first marriages over a forty-year period with a nearly 10 percent higher rate for second marriages.[4] Studies in countries where there were and still are many arranged marriages, such as mid-Eastern and Asiatic countries, reveal that there are "relatively few overall differences in marital satisfaction" between arranged marriages as compared with "love match" marriages, as explored in the book *Close Relationships* by Harold H. Kelley, et. al. Kelley discusses the results of a study of arranged Japanese marriages that indicated equivalent marital satisfaction or dissatisfaction whether the marriage was arranged by the family or directly by the man and woman involved.[5] So, whatever the method used to select a spouse, the success rate is very low. The unfortunate consequences affect children of all ages as well as the spouses.

Paradoxically, despite the far-reaching results of the marital decision, almost no one in Western civilization is provided any help, education or advice in choosing a mate. Neither high school nor college curricula have courses focused on spouse selection. It is difficult to locate videos, CDs or books with substantiated information that contain practical assistance in selecting a good match. Much of the help available concentrates on how to obtain dates, etc., but offers little on a proven plan for evaluating a potential partner and deciding to marry.

In the United States today and in most Western countries, the person one marries remains a choice based on highly emotional, illogical and often impulsive selection. In his groundbreaking book *Emotional Intelligence*, author Daniel Goleman states that the "raging" tyrant of lust can easily overcome the "solitary power" of reason.[6] This is a central tenet of our book and we hope to show why sex, no matter how enticing, should not be the central factor in pushing couples into unwise marriages. Meanwhile, author Erich Fromm, in his revealing book *The Art of Loving,* verifies the intractable nature of the quest for love. He explains "there is hardly any activity or enterprise which is started with such tremendous hopes and expectations, and yet which fails so regularly as love."[7]

We hope, by conveying the information, strategies and steps in this book, to help reduce the high incidence of divorce and to increase marital happiness. Our purpose is straightforward: to assist men and women in making more intelligent spouse choices. If men and women are more rational and less emotional in spouse selection and have a greater understanding of each other, there is a much higher probability that the marriages will succeed.

Our guide will help you evaluate a potential spouse. It is based on a thirty-five-item checklist covering a variety of factors that determine whether the person you are considering as a potential spouse is a good match and possesses the capacity to sustain a long-term committed relationship.

chapter one

Defining Love

L ove is an elusive goal sought by most of us. It is an emotional concept much discussed but little understood. The yearning for romantic love is pervasive. It permeates music, literature and drama. It is also the subject of endless discussion by most of us from adolescence through old age. Those who have experienced romantic love describe it as an altered state of being and feeling exhilarated, stimulated and complete. They feel they have found partners with whom, hand in hand, they will share a path to a fulfilling future.

In this book on spouse selection we take a careful look at the concept of love and what other experts have to say about this subject that occupies so much of our time and thought processes. About love, psychologist Nathaniel Branden observes: "Moved by a passion they do not understand for a goal they seldom reach, men and women are haunted by the vision of a distant possibility that refuses to be extinguished."[1] Perhaps this is the reason that psychologist Bernard Murstein said, "Without question, the major preoccupation of Americans is love."[2]

Social psychologists Stanton Peele and A. Brodsky argue in their book *Love and Addiction* that love can act as a "narcotic" with a mate providing a "quick fix" for everyday living problems.[3] Playwright George Bernard Shaw felt that "love is a game exaggerating the difference between one person and everybody" and H.L. Mencken, American journalist, editor and essayist, was equally satirical: "Love is the triumph of imagination over intelligence."[4]

A more positive and encouraging view of love is from psychologists Philip Shaver, Cindy Hazan and Donna Bradshaw, who convey that love relationships are similar to the "attachment" behavior between infant and parent in a "secure" parent/child relationship. They explain how an infant's need for "proximity with the parent as well as the cuddling, cooing, and tactile contact is very similar to the conduct of husband and wife in a good marriage."[5]

Psychologist George Levinger has explored the nuances of close relationships and commented on the need for reciprocity. He points out that "love's longevity depends on its mutuality."[6] Our research confirms the validity of this assertion. We believe no one would argue with the proposition that mutual affection powerfully and continually reinforces marital love. Other eminent authorities, in both the past and present, have focused upon the connection between sex and love. German physician Richard von Krafft-Ebing claimed that sexual desire apparently comes first in a relationship but that it diminishes or ends and is "replaced" by friendship.[7] English physician and famous sexologist Havelock Ellis came to a similar conclusion: love is "best viewed as a mixture of lust and friendship."[8] Further emphasizing the physical/sexual element of romantic love, Dr. Ellis states that sexual desire is an *important* part of romantic love.

Famed psychiatrist Sigmund Freud also seemed to be in accord, as noted in *The Nature and Pursuit of Love*: "To ensure a fully normal attitude in love, two currents of feelings have to unite— we may describe them as the tender, affectionate feelings and the sensual feelings."[9]

Psychologist Albert Ellis, the author of the book *The American Sexual Tragedy*, had quite a contrary view. He felt that "sated" sexual desire destroys the romantic love of modern courtship, leaving in its wake "calm, steady, enduring, domestic love."[10]

A number of social psychologists support the concept that romantic love and sex are related. They point out not only that "romantic love has become the *sine qua non* of the marriage contract," but also that "the absence of romantic love may be a factor in relationship dissolution" (i.e., divorce).[11] But we have not found any who echo the interesting opinion of Dr. Ellen Berscheid who affirms that love is "about 90 percent sexual desire as yet not sated." Dr. Berscheid writes that with "behaviors associated with romantic love, sexual arousal goes a long way."[12] And to further bolster the notion that sensual feelings have a definite niche in the vocabulary of romantic love, psychologist John Alan Lee states that the typical erotic lover is "eager to get to know the beloved quickly, intensely—and undressed."[13]

Nathaniel Branden agrees, in his concept of romantic love: a "passionate spiritual-emotional-sexual attachment between two people that reflects a high regard for the value of each other's person."[14] In fact, Dr. Branden implies that a relationship cannot even be viewed as romantic if it lacks a strong sexual element. While Dr. Branden does not quantify the importance of sex like Dr. Berscheid (and her "90 percent"), his concurring opinion certainly validates the important place of sex in love.

LOVE AND A LONG HEALTHY LIFE

Love is so intertwined with emotions and feelings that few people realize the connection between romantic love and a long, healthy life. Dean Ornish, MD, makes the astounding claim "Love and intimacy play a powerful role in our health, in our well being and even in our survival" and convincing scientific evidence supports this. In *Love and Survival,* Dr. Ornish details study after study showing love (like that experienced in good marriages) can prevent and sometimes even cure some of the most dangerous diseases.[15] It is not at all a stretch to conclude that a successful spouse hunt and a happy marriage will do much to promote a long, healthy life!

Most authorities confirm the fact that love is a combination—albeit somewhat complex—of physical, emotional and intellectual factors. Now let's take a closer look at some of these emotional and intellectual factors and consider how they relate to romantic love.

MARRIED LOVE: EMOTIONAL/INTELLECTUAL FACTORS

In our interviews with men and women who have been happily married for many years, both genders, regardless of their social and educational backgrounds, used almost identical terms when they responded to our request to describe their feelings about their long-term marriage partners, their relationships and their lives together:

- "I respect him."
- "I love her."
- "I have deep admiration for her."
- "He is someone with whom I feel safe and secure."
- "I have always 'looked up' to him."
- "I admire her integrity and honesty."
- "He is interesting and fun to be with."
- "I feel a great deal of pride, comfort and satisfaction about our life together."
- "I look forward to each day together with him."
- "We fight well together."
- "We enjoy each other's company."
- "She is my best and most trusted friend."
- "I am amazed how much I learn from my spouse."
- "I've always admired her good judgment; she is very level-headed."
- "He is very reliable; I can always count on him."
- "She has been a superb mother for our children."
- "He has been a good, loving and dutiful dad; the children and I have been very lucky."
- "She has such warmth and compassion!"

- "He has a lot of empathy; I know he really cares about me."
- "I respect his deep sense of morality and humanity."

Sexual and physical factors were *seldom* mentioned; nevertheless, there is good reason why the concept of physical attraction is most often associated with the idea of romantic love. Positive feelings such as admiration, pride and respect tend to increase sexual pleasure. Conversely, anger, distrust, suspicious feelings, insecurity and other negative feelings have the opposite effect. They will either inhibit or diminish sexual pleasure or, more usually, create resistance to engaging in any sexual activity. Animosity, distrust, coldness and other harmful feelings cast a negative aura over the entire marriage relationship. Pleasurable marital sex will suffer. If the married partners experience positive feelings for each other, their physical sexual relationship will be enhanced.

MALE-FEMALE DIFFERENCES IN SPOUSE SELECTION

The pathway to spouse selection may not be the same for both men and women. Let's explore their differences in approach in order that each may understand the other and become more tolerant and empathetic. What does each spouse seeker really want, both short-term and long-term? Then we will see how best to satisfy their desires.

What *He* Wants

Predominantly, the average young American male spouse seeker wants the rapture of frequent sex with an attractive, shapely, willing female. According to evolutionary psychologist David Buss's *The Evolution of Desire*, these sexual desires "are universal across cultures and are absent in none."[16] Men also want a compatible partner and companion. Most men realize if a woman is both willing and enthusiastic in bed and compatible, interesting and enjoyable out of bed, they will enjoy the relationship even more. In achieving sexual pleasure with a woman who is loyal to him and who also satisfies other needs, a man feels he has obtained the love he has always wanted and dreamed about: true, romantic and idealized. Love for this woman will grow and deepen with each successful sexual encounter. Slowly for some and rapidly for others, a man's love grows and matures, aided and abetted by a regular and satisfying sex life. Psychological researchers have found that such male focus on physical attractiveness, sex and loyalty is worldwide.

A man hopes and expects that this wonderful, fun-filled marital adventure will continue even after the arrival of children. In this way, he fantasizes how the right woman will continue to supply him with a satisfying life, both as wife and mother of their children. But we must understand that because of a man's more immediate and instinctive interest in the act of sex, his more mature and permanent appreciation of the "total" woman may not fully develop until later in the courtship period. Veteran actor Kirk Douglas is an excellent example of a male who had a preoccupation with sex. In speaking to *Life* magazine about a discussion with his wife, Anne, he wondered, "Gee, how did it all happen? When I met you, all I wanted was to get you into bed. Here, forty-four years later, we have two kids and two grandchildren."[17]

So far, we realize we have sketched a rather unflattering picture of the typical young American male. Is he really so focused on sex? Does he really give so little attention to the non-physical talents and abilities of his future lifetime mate? Is he really such a superficial, shallow, penis-centered lout, so obsessed with her crotch that he pays little attention to the long-range and, arguably, more important requirements of happy marriage? The answer is "yes" regarding many male spouse seekers. We hasten to add that the sex-obsessed male example we have described is not necessarily in the majority. But there is a lot of him in almost every man. It is best understood by recognizing the physiologic and historic fact that one typical male has the ability to impregnate hundreds of females. His awesome pro-creative powers (and his desire to utilize them) are probably traceable to prehistoric times, when infant death was the rule rather than the exception. Infant mortality remained very high well into the nineteenth century. Accordingly, nature programmed the male to be able to reproduce his germ plasma as often as possible. The sheer instinctive need for mankind to survive mandated repeated copulation: Discrimination was not a high priority from the male perspective.

It is undoubtedly true that both prehistorically and today there is competition among males for the more attractive females, although notions of chivalry, protection and even courtship have evolved. But the predominant force or theme between males and females, insofar as ancestral males were concerned, remained physical. Specifically, this translated into the urge to ejaculate, as often as possible, into many available females. As the evolutionary psychologists explain, males had to perform so to promote their own progeny.

Dr. Buss maintains that modern as well as ancient men want more sex with more women in order "to increase the number of their offspring" to preserve the species. He also states that while "in the business world time is money, in the mating world, time is sexual opportunity." And, he explains, the less time it takes to "score," the more offspring that can be produced. While it may be a stretch to saddle third millennium males with the libidinal habits of their prehistoric forebears, Dr. Buss and others in his field make a logical case for the proposition that this instinctive sexual force is still with us, albeit cloaked (to a degree) in more civilized garb.[18]

Nor did such male sexual programming undergo significant alteration when infant mortality improved (thanks to advances in modern medicine, better nutrition and more enlightened parental education). Even today, with most fetuses surviving pregnancy and birth, a man still carries with him the reproductive burden of bygone eras when men were fixated on sheer survival and could neither afford to consider nor appreciate the "total" woman and the benefits of her friendship and companionship along with the sexual satisfaction she supplied.

All psychologists do not wholeheartedly accept the theories of Dr. Buss and other evolutionary psychologists. There are a considerable number of female psychologists who do not agree with the proposition that today's man is fated to approach women like his prehistoric ancestor: fixated on repeated and indiscriminate copulation. This group (sometimes labeled social constructionists) believes that culture and environment need not be hobbled by ancient gender differences in attitudes toward sex and childcare. These psychologists, such as Alice Eagly at Northwestern University, point out that the human brain and social habit patterns are flexible and can adapt to this millennium. Eagly believes that the male's sexual preoccupation can be controlled by culture and environment.[19]

Nor are the differences among expert psychologists entirely gender based, although the male/female bias is definitely present. There are middle ground psychologists between Buss and Eagly. One of these is David Geary of the University of Missouri-Columbia, who admits there is "wiggle-room" between "caveman" sex notions and the modern "social constructionist" school. Nevertheless, says Dr. Geary, there are real biological differences that we must consider in this debate.[20]

In thinking about the quest for a spouse, we need not decide which school is correct. Insofar as the male is concerned, our task is to help him rise above his historic sexual shackles (if they exist) and learn how to select his lifetime mate more intelligently, so that both are better able to perform their four essential marital roles (chapter 3). Our checklist could prove useful in focusing a man's quest for a mate on those qualities that transcend the physical. Remember, in the thirty-five-item checklist we propose, only one item deals with sexual attraction (number 27).

What *She* Wants

Now let's take a close look at the average American female. Historically, how has she fared in her quest for a mate? Will she—can she—secure for herself the typical objective of most American females:

happy marriage with a lifetime mate who will fulfill both her romantic fantasies and practical needs? Will he make the necessary commitment? To answer these questions, we must analyze, from the female's perspective, her physiologic history, as well as both her conscious and unconscious contemporary desires.

A woman's desires are similar to those of a man's in some ways but significantly different in other areas. One of the differences is that her sexual "programming" differs quite radically from that of men's. As compared with men, a woman is far less focused on the sexual act. Usually she is much more globally involved in her prospective spouse and is interested in several different parts of his personality, strengths and weaknesses. She is concerned with how a prospective spouse feels about her emotionally and intellectually (as well as physically). Although she appreciates the erotic and physical attention from a man, she is equally (if not more) interested in his other feelings and actions toward her: Is he thoughtful, considerate, generous and compassionate? Will he take care of their children? Is he someone in whom she can feel pride? Does he earn an adequate income? What kind of lifestyle can he provide? Will he impart valuable genetic attributes such as intelligence, vigor and good health?

In her book *Sex on the Brain*, author and journalist Deborah Blum explains why a woman looks for a mate who will commit to her and with whom "she can share homebuilding and home defense, the rearing of the young, playing and cuddling." Blum explains how this (female) desire also permeates the gender throughout the animal kingdom.[21]

So we need to understand that women usually approach mate selection with priorities that differ from those of men. There is less emphasis on physical or sexual matters and more on intellectual, emotional and caretaking attributes.

WHY THE FEMALE MUST BE DISCRIMINATING
A woman's ability to reproduce and carry a pregnancy to term is severely limited as contrasted with a man's ability to impregnate.

After all, during her entire reproductive lifetime, a woman will produce only about four hundred eggs (one during each period of ovulation). But her male counterpart produces twelve million sperm per hour! He is capable of spawning hundreds of children. Nor is the male burdened with nine months of pregnancy followed by childbirth and its aftereffects. Thus the female *must* be more cautious and selective in her choice of the male whom she wants as a mate and father of her offspring.[22] Once she has allowed herself to be impregnated, she knows that the number of her births will be limited. It is also true that she is most vulnerable during pregnancy, childbirth and the postpartum period. So she must discriminate more carefully and select a man who will protect and care for her and their child. She knows her *quantity* of children may be small, compared with the huge procreative capacity of the male. Therefore, she must focus on *quality*. (Remember: the average United States family has 1.9 children!) This limitation of her ability to bear and raise children translates into several instinctive cautions.

- Caution about whom she should select as a father for her children. She understands the importance of a healthy, intelligent and compassionate mate if she is to produce children who will survive and prosper.
- Caution about the act of copulation itself. Even with modern birth control modalities, unplanned pregnancies occur. But as long as she is careful and refuses indiscriminate copulation, she better guarantees her continued ability to bear children fathered by a carefully chosen mate rather than with a male of dubious character, physically and otherwise.
- Caution about limiting her pool choices. She understands that if she has the ability to select from a larger pool of eligible males, she will have better odds of finding an optimum mate. So she must try to expand her pool of possible husbands (explored in chapter 6).
- Caution in protecting her reproductive ability that can easily be impaired by many sexually transmitted diseases (STDs).

Given the biological limitations of her seed and her consequent need to select a mate more carefully, what is on a woman's list for a potential mate?

- A spouse of whom she is proud and whom she admires; she expects him to have the same feelings about her.
- A spouse whom she respects and who shows her respect.
- A spouse whom she trusts and who will trust her.
- A spouse with whom there is mutual physical attraction.
- A spouse who will show her many years of affection and who will also be sensitive and attuned to her changing needs.
- A spouse who is committed to the relationship, does not abandon the family and remains faithful and loyal.
- A spouse who is interesting, companionable and a real friend.
- A spouse who will take care of her, protect her and supply emotional and physical support and financial security, which she feels is essential to their permanently married future.

All of this she wants from a husband whom she expects to love and cherish throughout her life. (Some of these desires and behaviors are discussed in more detail in chapter 3.)

We have explored male-female differences in the spouse selection process and it is clear that the process is complex, because it involves the union of two individuals with different life histories, personalities and genders. Marriage is not a static state, as both partners develop and grow. Nevertheless, couples can find their ways to developing secure, joyful long-term marriages despite differences, provided they utilize their powers of reason as well as their libidos.

MARRIAGE AND ITS REQUIREMENTS

A good marriage is a committed relationship based on love that endures: "until death do us part." This concept, as simple as it is appealing and the subject of many books, articles, songs, motion pictures, etc., expresses the desire of every couple who marries "for love." Authorities such as psychologists Havelock Ellis and Sigmund Freud, along with many others, agree that sex and friendship are integral parts of love. As Frank Sinatra sang: "Love and marriage go together like a horse and carriage." But stark, shocking and depressing reality collides with this idyllic definition, because many marriages now end in divorce. Many other marriages that appear to endure are equally unsuccessful, continuing to "flat line" for many years.

Our studies of current and past research and our experience with patients and clients plus our own long marriage point to the realistic solution we set forth in this book to remedy the sad state of this important institution. A stable marriage and its progeny form the bulwark of our society. We believe that more intelligent selection of spouses *before* marriage will markedly improve the prospects for long-term successful relationships *after* marriage, thus reducing the high incidence of divorce. We feel and have seen in our research, experience and studies that exploring and facing both positive and negative aspects of the behavior and history of a potential spouse before marriage will aid in spouse selection and help avoid stress and marital discord in the years to come.

chapter two

Examining a Relationship Without Structured Evaluation

We will focus on Joan and Gary, who followed a path to marriage based mostly on physical attraction and superficial social compatibility but who paid little attention to other vital information about each other. Although this example of Joan and Gary's whirlwind courtship and marriage may seem extreme, many unions take place between partners unaware of the personality characteristics and past histories of each other. The results reveal the probable collapse of their marriage.

Joan, twenty-five, was thrilled with her first date with Gary, twenty-seven. She loved the way Gary looked, dressed and spoke; she enjoyed his sense of humor. She felt that he was responsive to her as well. After a few dates she found herself thinking, *He is too good to be true.* Positive feelings grew as they attended classes at the same university while both were studying for their master's degrees in business administration. Eventually they were together most evenings and on the weekends. Their mutual physical attraction was powerful and, by their second month together, they were enjoying regular intimate sexual relations.

Joan and Gary had similar interests and intellects and came from the same socio-economic environment. Joan found pleasure in their stimulating social life at school. She noticed that Gary was often the "life of the party" at events like dances, teas, talks and town meetings. Their whirlwind romance continued and deepened. After three months Gary suggested a trip to Las Vegas, Nevada, where, he said, "I will have a surprise for you." So, during their next school break they headed for a four-day holiday, splurging by staying at one of the glamorous new hotels.

They checked into their luxurious room and while snuggling together in the afterglow of a delicious sexual interlude, Gary suggested that it was "time to check out the casino."

"After all," he said, " Vegas is where the action is."

Joan didn't know much about gambling, having played card games only a few times at the homes of friends; she knew little of craps. *But,* she thought as she watched Gary at the craps table, *I should learn a little about gambling since Gary seems to know his way around, judging by the way he is throwing the dice and calling out his moves.*

Joan was correct; Gary was not a novice. For a while he did very well and had a sizable and growing pile of chips. But since they had not eaten, Joan was getting hungry and said, "Come on, Gary, let's go eat. We can come back after dinner."

Gary pleaded for "just a few more throws—I'm on a roll."

"Well, okay," she said, "but only a few more!" But within five minutes, Joan noticed that Gary had lost his entire pile of chips. He walked away from the table disconsolate.

"I don't know what happened. Everything was going so great and then disaster! When I've come to Vegas in the past, I usually have better luck. But I guess you could say today I'm lucky at love, not at craps." He smiled ruefully.

Joan thought to herself, *I wonder how often he comes here to gamble.* But she kept quiet, not wanting to seem negative. She decided he needed some cheering-up and said, "Don't worry about it. We'll go to a show after we eat. I bet you'll have better luck and I guarantee you that when we get into bed a little later I'll make sure you'll have a lot of fun. You won't even remember those few bad moments. So, let's have a drink before dinner and forget all about your bad luck gambling at the craps table." This seemed to brighten Gary's spirits; he kissed Joan and they went to dinner. Joan noticed that Gary drank a martini before dinner and also ordered a bottle of wine with dinner, all of which he drank except for her one glass. She felt a twinge of concern about his drinking so much liquor, but then decided that it was okay, because he was not going to be driving his car anywhere.

Gary and Joan met some friends from their school for dinner the next evening. Joan noticed that Gary had two martinis before dinner and three or four glasses of wine with dinner. She made a mental note to ask him about his drinking but did not want to spoil things by acting like a nag. They had fun watching a performance by some amazing acrobats. Gary also went back to the craps table and did quite well, at first getting about one thousand dollars ahead then losing heavily. Later, when they were in bed, Gary told Joan, "The damn roof fell in. All of a sudden my luck turned. I lost every throw." Joan pressed her body against his and both smiled as they melted together blissfully, all else forgotten but their mutual pleasure. Before they drifted off to sleep, Gary whispered in her ear, "I have a question for you."

"What is it?" asked Joan.

Gary asked, "Will you marry me?"

Joan gasped and replied, "What a wonderful surprise! The answer is yes." All negative thoughts about Gary vanished. Joan had never felt so fulfilled. *As corny as it may sound*, she thought, *I feel like I'm entering the gates of heaven—and it's wonderful.* Concerns about money and Gary's drinking evaporated. They clung together joyfully, thinking of the many happy years ahead. They agreed that their wedding would take place in nine weeks, just after the college semester was over. She imagined herself in a bridal gown and veil. A formal wedding was something Joan had longed for since she was a teenager.

The next two months were filled with frenetic activity. Planning the wedding was not an easy task. They decided to have it at a hotel near Joan's house. Both of their families were happy to finance the event; they held many "conferences" to discuss details: the guest list, the food menu, the decorations and the officiant for the ceremony. Since both were Christians they decided on a young Methodist minister who headed the church Joan's family attended. Meanwhile, friends and family members were sending presents, including over five thousand dollars in checks. With Joan's consent, Gary put the funds in his checking account.

While all this activity kept both Joan and Gary busy, it nevertheless did not slow down their dates and parties, which were numerous over the next nine weeks. Although there was much work, including their MBA studies, there was also a lot of fun. Both Joan and Gary had their own apartments, but on most nights Joan stayed at Gary's. Their sex life continued regularly and both found it very satisfying.

Gary also attended his regular Friday night poker game with some male friends. These were high school buddies and Gary took Joan one Friday night to meet "the guys," all of whom told Gary he was a very lucky fellow. One of them said, "I hope I can find a gal like Joan someday." Joan noticed that there were several bottles of open scotch on the table and laughingly suggested to Gary, "Hey, don't drink too much. I don't want to see you racked up in an auto accident—or worse—and screw up our wedding plans!"

He reassured her, "Don't worry, sweetheart," as she left to attend a wedding shower given by her girlfriends.

Gary came home that night without incident and as they snuggled together in bed, Joan noticed that he smelled strongly of alcohol and that his speech was a little slurred. She said, "Don't you think it was dangerous driving home with all that scotch in you?"

Gary laughed. "Well, I made it, didn't I? And I promise you I'll be careful!" Reassured, Joan put her arms around him and their bodies melded in pleasure. As she drifted off to sleep, she thought, *Maybe I should put my foot down about this Friday night drinking?* But all was forgotten by the next morning.

Almost before they knew it, the wedding day was upon them. The wedding was beautiful and the post-ceremony party at a local hotel was great fun. Everyone gushed over the handsome couple and one guest grabbed the microphone and proposed a toast: "To the most beautiful bride and best-looking groom I've seen in the thirty years since I got married." Everyone applauded.

It was perfect, Joan thought as she and Gary drove to the airport, tin cans clanging behind the "Just Married" sign painted on their car in shaving foam. Soon they were on the airplane, headed to Hawaii for a week–long honeymoon. Their hotel overlooked the beach and the weather in Hawaii was wonderful: balmy with warm evenings. Days and nights were punctuated with delicious, mutually satisfying sex. They enjoyed relaxing and swimming. The week went by too quickly and soon the young couple arrived back at their newly furnished apartment on a Monday morning.

Everything was in order at their apartment, with one exception. There was no refrigerator. When Joan asked what happened, Gary said that he had no idea. He immediately called the appliance dealer where they had bought a brand new refrigerator.

"What's going on?" Gary asked. "Why wasn't it delivered like you promised?" The dealer explained that the credit card number Gary gave him two weeks earlier had been rejected and the dealer hadn't known how to reach Gary while the couple was away. Gary knew very well why his credit card had been rejected. He had "maxed it out" when he used it to pay half of his Las Vegas casino gambling debt. He took a deep breath and thought, *I'd better get that refrigerator right now.*

So Gary said, "Okay, I don't know what the credit card problem is, but just deliver it today and we'll pay on delivery." He was told the refrigerator would be delivered that afternoon and the bill was $485. "Okay," Gary said, "we'll be waiting." Gary knew there was still a problem. His checking account was close to zero. He hadn't told his new wife that he had used almost all the gift money—almost five thousand dollars—to pay the other half of his gambling debt at Las Vegas.

"Sweetheart," Gary said, "can you write out a check for the refrigerator?"

"Why don't you use the gift money? We couldn't have used up more than a thousand or so, if that," Joan replied.

Gary hesitated and then answered reluctantly, "Sweetheart, I was hoping I wouldn't have to tell you this, but I'm sorry to say I had to use up all except a couple hundred dollars to pay off what I owed to the Las Vegas casino."

Joan could hardly believe what she was hearing. "Do you mean to tell me all that money is just gone—the money we were expecting to use to finish furnishing our apartment?"

Gary was silent, not knowing what to say.

"Answer me!" Joan almost screamed. She felt herself beginning to lose control.

In a low voice, Gary said, "Yes. And I am really sorry; I know I shouldn't have done it without telling you, but I was hoping I could somehow replace the money soon so I wouldn't have to worry you."

Joan took a deep breath. She was afraid she was really going to "lose it." Then she had an idea and suggested, "Well, why not just put it on your credit card?"

Gary replied, "I would like to, but my credit card is also at its limit." He dreaded the question he was sure Joan would ask next.

"Maxed out? On what?" Joan asked. Now she was furious. "No, don't tell me. More evidence of your gambling problem that has gotten us into this mess."

Gary was too mortified to say anything, so he just nodded. Joan burst into tears, ran into the bedroom and lay on their bed sobbing.

PROBLEMS SUFFERED AND LESSONS LEARNED

We need go no further in the Gary/Joan saga to see that there is trouble ahead. As we will explain in chapter 3, gambling and/or alcohol are addictions that are often fatal to a marriage. These addictions can cloud mature decisions. Social controls evaporate. Anger in partners may go unchecked. Despite all of Gary's positive qualities, this marriage will most likely end in divorce. If it doesn't, it will be fraught with stress and conflict. Joan was unprepared for her disappointment in Gary. She did not foresee the effect of his gambling and perhaps drinking on their financial security. Unfortunately, Gary did not acknowledge that his drinking and gambling were problems. As a result, positive intervention in the form of individual or group therapy seems unlikely at this time.

What lessons might Joan learn from her unfortunate experience? It is essential to know as much as possible about a potential future spouse. Knowledge will enable an informed decision. But Joan failed to do this. She learned very little about Gary in the few months they were dating. Their whirlwind courtship did little to help her properly evaluate Gary's potential as a lifetime mate. There was a strong mutual physical attraction and a developing emotional bond, both of which impeded realistic assessment of Gary as a marital candidate. Also, Joan, as well as many mate seekers, had no structured approach or experience that would help her evaluate Gary as a potential husband. Joan noted Gary's excessive drinking and gambling; however, the combination of her lack of sophistication and the speed of the courtship obscured these problems.

We designed our Prospective Spouse Checklist to supply spouse seekers with a more realistic evaluation of a prospective partner's behavior and personality and to help determine how he or she will fulfill the four marital roles of friend, lover, parent and business partner. After we consider the checklist we will have the opportunity to see what happens with a second and much different Joan/Gary example. In essence, we will rewrite the history of this couple (the way it should have been) and explain how Joan should have handled her relationship with Gary. Joan will utilize the Prospective Spouse Checklist, which provides her with a structure to help her evaluate Gary, and you will see how Joan approaches spouse selection using the knowledge she acquires from the checklist. The checklist factors she considers give her the confidence to arrive at an informed decision concerning Gary and his marriage proposal.

chapter three

Understanding the Prospective Spouse Checklist and Its Function

We created the Prospective Spouse Checklist as a guide to help men and women make the most important decision of their lives: should you marry this person with whom you are involved? Often, initial physical attraction as well as the intense desire to form a relationship and have a partner prevent spouse seekers from making rational evaluations of prospective lifetime mates. Also, many spouse seekers indulge in wishful thinking and "endow" prospective marital partners with qualities that they do not really have. In fact, prior to marriage most of us are not even aware of the many essential areas that should be considered before deciding upon the selection of a marital partner.

To achieve a marriage that provides joy, satisfaction and security we provide the thirty-five questions on the checklist, which must be answered, separately, for each member of the couple. The answers to these questions will help determine if a prospective mate will fulfill the four major roles that each spouse must perform in an enduring relationship:

- Friend/companion/adviser
- Lover and sexual partner
- Parent (if there are children)

- Lifetime business partner (in a partnership that can never be dissolved once there are children)

The checklist will also help to determine if a prospective spouse is able to properly fulfill the two requirements for a successful marriage:
- Possess the emotional capacity to make and sustain an exclusive lifetime commitment to a mate.
- Be a good match for his/her mate.

Our checklist supplies a structure to use in the selection and evaluation of both prospective spouses. It will help to determine if each is able to meet the two requirements and properly perform his or her four marriage roles. We concede this is not a simple task and that it will require both members of the couple to devote more time and cerebral effort to an enterprise that has seemed to receive—so far—too much emotion and far too little rational consideration.

We suggest that you look over the checklist but wait to give it detailed consideration until you read the explanatory material concerning each item. Then, go back and look more closely at each of the items. Understanding these factors will help you to make a decision about choosing your prospective spouse, a person who is a "four-in-one" mate, has the capacity to commit to a permanent relationship and is a good match for you.

THE PROSPECTIVE SPOUSE CHECKLIST

Use a separate list for each person. Although there is no pass/fail score, more "YES" checks and fewer "NO" checks point to better odds for marital success.

Note we have marked ten of the items with asterisks (*). Each of these items is a red flag and should be considered very carefully. A "NO" check mark for any of these ten items is serious and should be meticulously explored.

BASIC INFORMATION	YES	NO
*1. SINGLE		
2. NO CHILDREN		
3. NO PREVIOUS MARRIAGE		
4. SMALL AGE DIFFERENCE		
5. SIMILAR EDUCATION		
6. SIMILAR INTELLIGENCE		
7. SAME RACE, RELIGION AND CULTURE		
8. ADEQUATE OR POTENTIAL ASSETS/INCOME		
FAMILY HISTORY	**YES**	**NO**
*9. WELL TREATED, LOVED AND NURTURED IN EARLY YEARS		
10. SAME CAREGIVER(S) TO AGE THREE		
11. PARENTS REMAINED MARRIED THROUGH TEEN YEARS		
*12. GOOD RELATIONSHIPS WITH PARENTS, SIBLINGS AND GRANDPARENTS		
13. OBSERVED AFFECTION BETWEEN PARENTS		
14. PARENTS: GOOD PHYSICAL/EMOTIONAL HEALTH, NO MAJOR ALCOHOL, DRUG OR OTHER PROBLEMS		
PERSONALITY TRAITS/BEHAVIORS	**YES**	**NO**
15. KIND AND CONSIDERATE		
16. SENSE OF HUMOR		
17. CHEERFUL		
18. HAS FRIENDS		
19. MATURE JUDGMENT		

	YES	NO
20. FLEXIBLE		
21. PROMPT		
22. ORGANIZED AND NEAT		
*23. ABLE TO CONTROL ANGER		
24. WILLING TO ACCEPT ADVICE		
25. GENEROUS		
MUTUAL ELEMENTS OF COMPANIONSHIP	**YES**	**NO**
*26. ENJOY TIME TOGETHER		
*27. SEXUAL ATTRACTION		
*28. AGREEMENT ON MORAL, ETHICAL AND POLITICAL ISSUES		
*29. AGREEMENT ON MAJOR GOALS: HAVING A FAMILY, RELIGIOUS AFFILIATION, CHILDCARE		
30. AGREEMENT ON MONEY MANAGEMENT AND INVESTMENTS		
31. AGREEMENT CONCERNING PETS		
32. ACCEPTANCE OF MATCH BY BOTH FAMILIES		
OTHER PROBLEM AREAS	**YES**	**NO**
*33. NO ADDICTION TO SMOKING, ALCOHOL, DRUGS OR GAMBLING		
*34. NO MAJOR PHYSICAL, MENTAL OR EMOTIONAL HEALTH PROBLEMS		
35. NO MAJOR PAST OR PRESENT LEGAL PROBLEMS		
TOTALS		

THE "FOUR-IN-ONE" SPOUSE

Let's now examine the four roles of each spouse as well as the two essential spouse requirements: capacity to commit and being a good match.

After a few dates, most people usually come to some general conclusions concerning the other party as a prospective spouse: he or she is attractive or unattractive, we had fun together or were bored, I like the person and will continue dating or I do not and will end the relationship. However, this approach is much too simplistic. We suggest you need to take a closer look at the other person, particularly if the ultimate objective is marriage. Your prospective lifetime spouse should be able to fulfill four separate roles. Even more challenging, each of these parts is usually performed concurrently in the years ahead. Let's look at each role separately.

FRIEND/COMPANION/ADVISOR

You and your spouse-to-be should be good friends who find each other interesting, responsive, helpful and fun outside the bedroom. You should feel comfortable spending much time together alone, enjoying each other's company, sharing mutual values, goals and activities and responding to each other's needs and desires. Humor and laughter are part of the shared experiences. Listening to each other's anxieties, rants and sobs defines the role of a good friend. A companion and advisor will impart wisdom, comfort, information and advice which also enrich the relationship.

One of our couples, Joe and Mary, exhibits this combination of blending roles, interests, opinions and feelings.

Joe was an accountant, but at home he enjoyed woodworking and had a complete workshop. He and Mary had been married for over twenty-five years, during which time he had made tables, chairs and various items of furniture that both he and Mary enjoyed.

However, their interests were amazingly different. Mary liked to read. Joe did not. Mary read both fiction and nonfiction and her reading consumed much of her time when she was not working at the library. Although they both worked full-time, Mary and Joe spent most evenings and weekends together. There were many occasions when Mary stopped reading and Joe also left his workshop and they sat together enjoying cups of tea. At these times, Mary explained to Joe the plot of the novel she was reading or if the book was nonfiction, she discussed the author's subject and point of view. Joe, although a non-intellectual, was intelligent and analytical and enjoyed these interchanges with Mary. The feeling was mutual. Mary spent long hours with friends, both in person and on the telephone, so she enjoyed sharing tidbits of gossip with Joe. These topics varied widely, from what was occurring in their hometown to what was happening with their own children and their friends' children, many of whom were in college. She often asked Joe's advice dealing with problems that arose in their extended family and the community.

Joe never hesitated to ask Mary's opinion on financial matters as they planned for future expenditures, trips and household improvements or regarding special problems he was having with one of his current projects.

Joe and Mary had a very satisfying sex life. But aside from that and despite quite different interests, they seemed to be very compatible and were good friends and companions.

The satisfying relationship of Joe and Mary is an example of how two people, though different in many aspects, can come together and find happiness despite dissimilar strengths, personalities and interests.

The courtship and engagement period is the best time to determine whether or not you and your possible spouse find each other interesting and compatible. The couple should utilize this timespan and not hurry the process. There should be no hard and fast time limits on the length of an engagement. If the partners meet frequently and engage in many different activities for five or six months, they may feel confident that they have filled the roles of friends and companions. If there are long separations between dates, more time may be required so the couple can reflect on and eventually answer with confidence these questions: Do we enjoy each other's company? Can we be good friends to each other? If you are uncertain about the answers to these questions even after a long engagement, consider one of two possible courses of action:

- Discontinue the relationship and look elsewhere.
- Postpone the marriage, extend the engagement period and allow yourself time to determine if he or she fulfills the role of good friend and companion.

Of the four spouse roles, the good friend is probably the most important. It is the essential "glue" that will keep the marriage together and functioning for its many years and create an abiding attachment. A corollary function is that of a 24/7 advisor on every conceivable topic ranging from what tie or dress to wear to a party to whether to accept a lucrative job in a distant city. Listening to and accepting advice is also part of the equation that is involved in being a good friend. The Prospective Spouse Checklist will help you determine if your future mate will function as required by this first role (see discussion of checklist items 15: Kind and Considerate, 17: Cheerful, 24: Willing to Accept Advice and 26: Enjoy Time Together).

LOVER AND SEXUAL PARTNER

A good marriage usually requires a mutually satisfying sex life. This adds the zest, flavor and intimacy that cannot easily be supplied by other means. Recognizing and responding to both partners' sexual needs and appetites is an important force in promoting a healthy marriage. Sexual behaviors and needs usually change after marriage, after childbirth or with age. How a wife or husband responds when the courtship period ends often depends upon the spouse's ability to be sensitive, nurturing and empathetic. This is also related to the ability to both give and receive affection. But the very exhilaration of sexual arousal and erotic pleasure in the courtship period often overpowers reason and prevents spouse seekers from carefully considering the many other non-sexual factors that will make or break the marriage. Most marital authorities agree that sex, although essential, comprises only a minor percentage of the total requirements of successful marriage. (Checklist item 27 is the only one that deals with sex.)

Physical attraction produces the energy and motivation for most developing attachments. Let's discuss Robin and Jake, who illustrate how partners discover, over time, whether this essential ingredient is present in their relationships.

Robin met Jake in a chemistry laboratory at the local university. They were both seniors living at home and commuting. Robin, who was attracted to Jake, found herself staring at him while he concentrated on carefully measuring liquid into a beaker. Jake happened to look up and smiled as their eyes met. To her surprise, he asked her to help him in calculating and recording some data for his experiment. After working side by side entering information in his lab book, he offered to help Robin with her lab assignment. Robin had already finished, so she suggested, "I'm hungry; let's have a bite to eat."

That "bite to eat" developed into a warm friendship. They began sharing rides to campus and meeting in the library after classes to work on assignments. Eventually they made a date to go to the movies on the weekend. They were physically attracted to each other but had not found the time or place to explore that intimate part of their relationship. For Robin, their spontaneous, casual hugging and kissing was thrilling and the anticipation of greater intimacy was intense.

As Robin and Jake's relationship continued, they found that they were very compatible, both as lovers and as companions. They had much in common and enjoyed being together and discussing all types of topics. They were also a good match in terms of values and goals. Eventually, on an overnight camping trip, they were able to be sexually intimate and to explore each other erotically. Their sex was extremely pleasurable and fulfilling and seemed to cement their developing attraction, bond and friendship.

In addition to their initial attraction, Robin and Jake had common ground because of their mutual interest in science. Not every such encounter will lead to enjoyable sex, but this couple exhibits mutual fulfillment of two of the four essential spouse roles. In this couple's relationship we see the beginnings of a good foundation for a healthy partnership.

PARENT

If a couple has children, the many arduous years of childrearing require two conscientious parents to love and nurture the children and be responsive to their growing needs. Although an increasing number of children live in single family homes, most children do better and thrive in a well-functioning nuclear family where both parents are present and participating in their respective roles. In her *Time* article "Is There Hope for the American Marriage?" Caitlin Flanagan discusses current marriage/divorce problems in the United States. Flanagan explains that children require two parents and suffer in their development if they grow up without a father at home in a well-functioning family.[1]

Our checklist contains a number of items that will help determine if the possible mate will be a nurturing and responsible parent.

How we have been parented has a great influence on how we will respond to our children. As psychiatrist John Bowlby said, "We do unto others as we have been done by."[2] This is why it is so essential to explore the family history of a prospective spouse, which is covered in checklist items 9 through 14. Unfortunately, we cannot always observe during courtship how a spouse will behave toward a son or daughter.

When a partner has a child or children from a previous marriage, the role of stepparent is also important. Is the prospective stepparent willing and able to successfully function in the role of parent to a child who is not united to him or her by biological ties? Whether we consider our own children or stepchildren, our attitudes and behaviors toward them will need to be explored during the period of courtship and engagement. Attitudes regarding discipline and negative behavior may differ with each partner and become a cause of future conflict.

Unfortunately, many marriages take place because of unexpected pregnancy and couples are catapulted into the role of parents soon after the wedding. Such marriages may unite couples for the wrong reason. The spouses may be poorly matched and unable to fulfill the essential roles required. Often, many problems are created, all of which bode ill for the (forced) marriage. Our book focuses, however, on marriages entered into willingly by both parties who have the opportunity to reflect on their choices without time or other constraints.

Another facet of the good parent requirement is the "times of need" in every husband-wife relationship when one marital partner needs nurturing, kindness and empathy. Such needs may arise when circumstances have created stress, illness or exhaustion. It is therefore wise to determine, prior to marriage, whether a potential spouse possesses such capacities. The Nurturing Checklist in chapter 5 further explains how couples can parent and tend to each other's needs, while at the same time investing in the relationship. The courtship period is an appropriate time to observe these qualities.

LIFETIME BUSINESS PARTNER

This partnership is affected by the earnings and spending habits of both parties. Over the years a large amount of money comes in and goes out. The business partnership is complex and very long-term. If there are children it will last a lifetime regardless of whether or not the couple divorces. Because of commitment to their children and grandchildren, mother and father are permanently tied together financially.

This marital financial enterprise is far more complex and may create more potential problems than an ordinary business partnership. It requires all the acumen essential to any enterprise, along with the need to be both flexible and generous. After all, the most talented CEO and CFO could have trouble allocating limited income to competing family expense requirements, such as a second car, a large tuition or another child. Checklist items such as item 19: Mature Judgment and other personality traits contained in items 15 through 25 should be seriously considered. Many of these, like item 22: Organized and Neat or item 25: Generous, will affect the operation of this marital financial enterprise and can influence and even determine whether or not the marriage will function successfully. When selecting a spouse ask yourself: Will he or she be a good business partner? An adequately long courtship should provide an opportunity to discover whether the candidate exhibits compulsive spending, saving or gambling behaviors, as well as the potential to earn a living, hold a job and wisely manage the finances during the years of marriage.

Another of the couples we studied, Stan and Charlotte, wrestled with financial tensions and disagreements but were able to resolve them.

Stan and Charlotte were eagerly anticipating their forthcoming marriage. Their year-long engagement had been a time of pleasure, particularly during the months they were living together. Both felt that they were fortunate to have met, even though things had been turbulent prior to their engagement. At that time they had resolved what had seemed to be an intractable problem: Stan's inability to control his impulses to spend money on clothes, electronic gadgets and expensive French wines. This had put considerable stress on their budget and had driven Charlotte to distraction. When the overspending became obvious, Charlotte was very disturbed. It was their only real source of conflict.

Charlotte was interested in money matters and enjoyed handling money, balancing her checkbook and keeping track of their retirement accounts. Saving, seeing her bank account grow, gave her pleasure. In addition, her college degree was in economics and accounting and she understood the financial issues facing a young couple.

One day the issue resurfaced and after bickering at the mall, Stan admitted that he had a problem with controlling his spending and needed help. "Why don't you take over and handle our money?" he suggested after some thought. "You can even put me on an allowance and I promise I will stick to it. You are good with money and I don't like fighting about it."

Stan's acknowledgement of his part in their conflict and his respect for Charlotte's ability and interest as a business partner seemed to resolve the tension. The allowance suggestion worked.

It was helpful that Stan and Charlotte openly discussed the issues involving money and finances instead of arguing over it. They were better prepared to understand and assess how each of them would fulfill the role of business partner in their marriage.

Even assuming that a spouse is able to adequately perform the four roles just discussed, does she or he possess the capacity for a permanent commitment? Is he or she a good match for you? We will examine each of these issues. Keep in mind that the checklist items, which we will consider in some detail, will also help to answer these important questions.

THE COMMITMENT REQUIREMENT

One of our clients, Linda, has been in a "relationship" with a man for three years. They have even moved in together. Sex is great and frequent. But she can't seem to get him to propose. She told her girl-friends, "I don't know. He's great, but when I bring up the subject of marriage or children he gets this frightened look in his eye and changes the subject. Or, sometimes, there is vague talk of settling down 'someday.' I get the feeling that maybe he just can't or won't commit." This is a scenario we have heard many times from clients and friends. Linda is rightfully concerned, because the ability and willingness to form a permanent commitment is absolutely crucial for an enduring marriage. This is why it is vital to choose a prospective mate who will be able to sustain such a relationship as well as commit to marriage.

To determine whether or not a prospective mate has this capacity, we must look into the person's early relationships and understand their profound influence on the person's adult behavior. We will discover why some adults can commit and others cannot.

THOSE WHO CAN COMMIT

Early childhood relationships and experiences can seriously affect adults' ability to form and sustain loving attachments. Such early experience is rarely considered or explored, but it is profoundly important (refer to checklist items 9 to 14). Human beings and animals learn to love, because they have been loved and nurtured in their first years of life. It is during this early (preverbal) period that they learn to trust that their new world is safe and protected and that they will be fed when hungry, comforted when sad and stimulated when bored. They feel comfortable and reassured by having the same few caregivers with the same arms, the same smells, the same voices, the same songs and even the same predictable methods of holding and feeding. Infants and toddlers need to feel close proximity to those who care for them.

Through responsive nurturing during the infant years, children develop a sense of optimism and feel that they are valued. As a result of continuous and positive nurturing care, a secure attachment or bond forms between child and caregiver(s). This is the beginning of the child's capacity to experience a loving relationship.[3]

These positive feelings about a caregiver are transferred to teachers, friends, other adults and ultimately to a lifetime mate. As psychologists Shaver, Hazen and Bradshaw explain, the attachment bond and commitment between infant and caregiver formed so early in life is very similar to the bond of trust and love that forms between husband and wife in a good marriage, where each nurtures, cares for and is committed to the other—just as a mother cares for her infant. An infant or toddler derives joy and satisfaction from his or her mother or other primary caregivers. As adults, husband and wife may also enjoy giving and receiving pleasure from each other.[4] The child learns to trust and love at the very beginning of life and he or she is able to transfer that affection to a spouse. Therefore, the capacity to commit and function as a loving mate has its roots in these critical childhood years. Positive early attachments form a template for later secure relationships.

A securely attached adult might describe how he or she feels when relating to others. A person like this may report something such as, "It is relatively easy to get close to others. I am comfortable depending on them or having them rely on me. I am not concerned about being left out or abandoned or even about a person getting too close to me."

THOSE WHO CANNOT COMMIT

Let's consider the reasons why some possible mates either cannot commit or may have difficulty in doing so. We will also consider how you can determine who they are and what might be done to remedy this problem.

In order to identify a prospective spouse who cannot commit it is essential to look into the early childhood years just as we did in the section about those who can commit. In that discussion we revealed how a positive nurturing environment in the early years helps to develop a mature adult who has the capacity to sustain a long and happy marriage. Conversely, a negative and non-responsive or abusive environment can produce the opposite result, because the unfortunate infant may learn a much different message: that it is too dangerous to trust and rely upon caregivers and others and that his or her new world is not safe, nurturing and protective. These feelings may stem from caregivers who are non-responsive, punishing, abusive, neglectful or constantly changing.[5]

It is very difficult for infants to feel safe and secure if caregivers constantly come and go. Such children are victims of "caregiver roulette," never knowing in whose arms they will land. They experience no sense of continuity or predictability, even though each (changing) caregiver may be very positive and conscientious. Instead of forming a secure attachment and positive bond with one caregiver after another, a child with such a history may become suspicious, wary and anxious and develop the conviction that it is too dangerous to trust, love and invest in a committed alliance. Some of these children may feel that they can only rely upon themselves for safety, satisfaction and pleasure. In adolescence or adulthood they may turn to alcohol or drugs to provide stimulation and soothing as a substitute for the nurturing they did not receive when they were very young.[6] As adults they may feel that commitment to an enduring and committed relationship may be "too dangerous" to attempt, because they feel the adults in their childhoods failed them.

Adults with this kind of history may have difficulty committing to a relationship. If they are able to verbalize their feelings they may admit: "I am afraid of becoming too close to others. It is hard to trust them completely. I get anxious when I have to rely or depend on others. I feel like escaping when I am expected to become more intimate than I feel I can."

Twenty or more years separates such early negative experiences from the period of dating, courtship, engagement and marriage. As explained in the discussion about those who can commit, it may be difficult to accept the concept that there is a causal connection between such early events and relationships and marital failure many years later. But such conclusions are well established. It can be considered as an unfortunate and delayed "time bomb" effect.

The checklist items in the Family History section (items 9 through 14) are designed to help the spouse seeker explore these commitment issues so that the seeker can determine into which of these two categories the prospective spouse fits. Will he or she, because of negative events in infancy or childhood, have problems in making a permanent commitment? Does the possible mate have a positive attachment and bonding history which would indicate that he or she possesses the capacity for an enduring commitment?

In order to answer "YES" or "NO" on these Family History items, particularly numbers 9 and 10 that deal with the earliest years, it may be necessary to obtain information from other sources such as friends, family members and relatives. This should be done carefully and diplomatically. Over time, in casual conversation, important information can usually be obtained without difficulty. It is during dating and courtship that partners look at underlying aspects of their future mates. (We discuss this concept further in chapter 5.)

Spouse seekers should not overreact and automatically disqualify a marital prospect because of a negative or even abusive history as a child. As psychologist and researcher Judith Wallerstein explains in *The Good Marriage,* there are many examples of happy and long-term marriages despite a very negative attachment and bonding history on the part of one or both partners.[7] Human beings can be amazingly resilient and some are able to avoid emotional damage despite negative childhood events.

Perhaps, with such prospects, there were reparative or thera-peutic relationships during adolescence or young adulthood. Or per-haps some were able to gain insight because of professional intervention. Others may have had relationships with good friends or teachers who were sympathetic, understanding and who provided helpful insight. Grandparents may have played a vital role in a child's life. They may have spent more quality time with their grandchildren and provided more predictable support as compared to parents who were often absent or abusive. Or there may have been aunts or uncles who were protective, nurturing and stimulating. So it is certainly advisable to consider all such possibilities and avoid making quick judgments that may disqualify an otherwise promising spouse prospect.

If there is concern that a possible spouse still appears to be affected by early childhood neglect or abuse, inquiry can be made if he or she is receptive to the idea of professional help. The time for such considered exploration, as we've discussed, is during the period of dating and courtship, when there is opportunity to explore such early childhood events and observe how the prospective spouse reacts and relates over an extended period of time. Our checklist provides a structure containing issues and behaviors that each spouse searcher should keep in mind during this period of observation and evaluation.

THE GOOD MATCH REQUIREMENT

In addition to the commitment requirement, spouse seekers need to evaluate potential spouses to determine whether each is a good match for the other. This process is highly subjective and individual. Since two people are involved, it is important not only to evaluate their respective behaviors, traits and attitudes, but also to determine how they will "mesh" and whether or not they will remain compatible during many years of marriage. It is important to explore one's own needs and behaviors as well as to learn what can be expected and tolerated in a prospective partner.

Researchers Walter Toman and William Cane studied successful marriages. They wanted to determine what seemed to create a "good match." They postulated that there were special personality characteristics associated with being an only child, first born, middle or youngest child and explored the effects of birth order on marital compatibility.[8] These broad general observations include many of the behaviors, attitudes and traits featured on our checklist.

Dr. Toman explains that spouses are happiest and are potentially a good match if they marry someone with similar characteristics to the sibling or siblings in their families of origin. For example, a firstborn female in a family of boys will be happiest marrying the lastborn son of a family with sisters. The firstborn female will have extensive experience in relating to and perhaps managing her younger male siblings. Likewise, the lastborn male will have had many years living with his older sisters. He will have learned how to cope with them as they exerted their influence upon him.

Children with no siblings may have specific strengths and deficits. They may be highly motivated and success-oriented but have a hard time being flexible, listening and receiving advice. They lack the experience of relating to peers as compared to growing up in a family with siblings.

Adults from a family of either all boys or all girls may have difficulty relating to a partner since they didn't grow up in a household with the opposite sex. The eldest son of an all-boy family may have difficulty if he marries the eldest daughter of an all-girl family. Theoretically, both were leaders in their home environments and may have difficulty in relinquishing their authority during the give and take required in marriage.

Middle children may be most flexible, having had to deal with both older and younger siblings.

Whereas these general observations may well be clinically valid, dating experience seldom includes marital prospects who neatly fit one of Toman's birth order categories. In the end, to help evaluate the good match potential of a mate, it is important to explore the specific items on the checklist. Unlike the commitment requirement discussed, which mainly concerns checklist items 9 through 14, the good match requirement actually requires consideration of all thirty-five items. If a female prospect was badly abused as a young child and has the potential to abuse her own children (item 9), she may be a very poor match regardless of her birth order. A male may be a poor match if he rates a "NO" for Able to Control Anger (item 23). So may a couple if the partners find that their values and goals differ. Other poor match examples may be a thirty-year age difference, great disparity in educational levels and lack of physical or sexual attraction. The same poor match conclusion may be reached if a partner has serious legal issues (item 35). If your marital prospect has had some run-ins with the law and repeated conflicts in the workplace, the "warning flag" should be up. This is true even if he or she seems to have a perfect birth order fit.

In considering the good match requirement, we realize that some of the checklist items may seem obvious: drinking, drug addiction, agreement on children, etc. But most couples either fail to consider many risk items or, if they do think of them, they fail to carefully consider how the negatives will affect their future relationships. We also recognize that having to weigh and consider thirty-five items may seem to be daunting and difficult. You may even feel that the entire checklist process is too cold and clinical and that you might be better off letting your heart or your gut tell you what to do. We feel that your future happiness requires that you use structured assessment and insight for your future relationship plans. That is the rationale of our book: the heat of erotic passion, the development of attachment and the wonderful flush of love needs to be tempered with continuing observation and evaluation.

No one is perfect and it will ultimately become necessary, after considering all "YES" and "NO" items, to decide whether you are willing to live with the negatives. It will be important to explore the strengths and weaknesses of each potential partner and to attempt to look many years ahead to help you make your decision.

A long courtship and engagement, at least six to twelve months, is advisable to supply you with the time necessary to gather and reflect on the information needed to make this crucial decision. Our checklist is designed to help accomplish this admittedly difficult task, so that the good match requirement is properly fulfilled.

The good match is probably the most basic husband-wife requirement. In *Good People, Bad Marriages*, author Marsha Lee Hudgens is unequivocal in her opinion of the necessity of a couple being a good match and states that there is no fixing a bad marriage if it is not a good match.[9] We agree! But if there are children, divorce is not the most attractive option; the children and their futures deserve equal consideration. We conclude that it is a very good idea to attempt to determine if it is a good match *before* you marry and certainly before there are children. If such a negative determination is made before children, divorce may be the most attractive option.

RED FLAG ITEMS
Ten of the checklist items are critically important. Each of these items is marked with an asterisk on the checklist:
- Item 1: Single
- Item 9: Well Treated, Loved and Nurtured in Early Years
- Item 12: Good Relationships with Parents, Siblings and Grandparents
- Item 23: Able to Control Anger
- Item 26: Enjoy Time Together
- Item 27: Sexual Attraction
- Item 28: Agreement on Moral, Ethical and Political Issues
- Item 29: Agreement on Major Goals: Having a Family, Religious Affiliation, Childcare
- Item 33: No Addiction to Smoking, Alcohol, Drugs or Gambling

- Item 34: No Major Physical, Mental or Emotional Health Problems

Note that these items affect both the commitment and good match requirements, as well as indicating whether a prospective spouse will be able to fulfill his or her four roles. We suggest you read our explanations of these items carefully. Each of them poses such grave concerns that we caution anyone to think most seriously before committing to a long-term relationship with a person who rates a "NO" on any of these red flag items.

ANSWERING THE CHECKLIST ITEMS

Begin filling out the "YES" and "NO" answers to the thirty-five item checklist as soon as the dating process begins, providing you decide that you feel he or she may be a marital candidate. Some of the information will require time to obtain. Many items should be apparent after the first few dates, such as the items in the Basic Information section. However, other items, such as those in the Family History category, may require more time to answer. As you record answers concerning your potential mate, keep in mind the necessity to explore these items for yourself and to record a check mark in the appropriate "YES" or "NO" box in addition to the check marks for your intended. Some of these answers will be easy for you, because you know your history and have some insight into your personality characteristics. But answers to items in the Mutual Elements of Companionship and Other Problem Areas categories may need weeks or months to determine and will require discussion with your possible future partner.

To what extent should one engage the prospective spouse in the process of considering the checklist? With each relationship a decision should be made: Either explore the items of the list together as a couple or complete the list privately, saying nothing to the other person. Some new partners may feel threatened by the checklist concept, whereas others may readily embrace the process. In the end, the decision of whether or not to disclose the existence of the check-list must be made individually.

As you consider your checklist answers (for both you and your intended), try to remain as objective as possible. During the courtship period do not hesitate to change answers from "YES" to "NO" or vice versa if you feel that a correction is called for by facts that are revealed as you and your partner continue in your relation-ship. As you continue your search for a spouse, you will probably dis-cover that most potential partners, no matter how attractive, will rate "NO" on a number of the factors. Overall, the most important ques-tion should be: Realizing that very few prospects will score "YES" on all items, can I live happily with these negatives?

In chapter 4 we will recast the Joan and Gary relationship we previously discussed. In our new plotline we will watch Joan use our checklist as she handles her relationship with Gary more rationally. Before we see how Joan accomplishes this, let's look at each of the checklist items that Joan needs to consider.

BASIC INFORMATION

The first eight checklist items are the easiest to assess early in the courtship period. During conventional dating most partners will question each other as to their marital status. If married or divorced, do they have children? What schools have they attended? What is the nature of their work if employed? Age and racial differ-ences may be easily observed. Some of this information can be obtained over the phone or by online communication even before the spouse seekers decide to meet. Much time can be saved by elim-inating prospects who may not be acceptable per a spouse seeker's qualifying factors.

*1. SINGLE

Ordinarily, a married person should not be considered as a future spouse. Occasionally there may be exceptions, such as someone who is in the process of getting divorced. A person who is only separated should not be considered a prospective partner, because the divorce may never take place. Too often people waste time in relationships with married partners who talk about getting divorced but who never manage to see it through. Unless the divorce takes place promptly and verifiably, a current marriage should be enough to disqualify a person as a realistic prospect. Remember this is a red flag item.

Tanya and Howard are another couple we looked at more closely:

> Tanya met Howard at a church social and thought he had dating possibilities. Both Tanya and Howard had gone to college, were well read and enjoyed hiking, the outdoors and other mutual interests. During their second date, Howard mentioned that although he was still married, he was living separately and was going to be divorced in the "near future." When Tanya asked how long he had been separated, Howard replied, "A little over a year. I hope it moves along faster."
>
> Tanya asked, "What's the delay?"
>
> Howard replied, "We have a son and we have not been able to agree on visitation rights and a few other issues, like the amount of child support. I have a good lawyer and I hope to wrap this up soon."

Tanya has some important decisions to make. Should she wait until the divorce is concluded to date Howard? When children are involved, reconciliation can occur and it is possible Howard may never finalize his divorce. Is Tanya ready and willing to be a stepmother and handle the custody and visitation matters associated with this role? Is it wise for Tanya to start married life with such complications? It may be sensible for Tanya, who is a young spouse seeker, not to settle for Howard. At present, she is able to meet a variety of young, unattached men.

2. NO CHILDREN

A potential spouse who has a son or daughter poses several marital risks. Falling in love with someone does not necessarily mean you will have a positive relationship with his or her child, nor does it mean that your prospective partner will have a positive relationship with your own child. Even though both members of the couple may genuinely enjoy and accept their new stepchildren, there is no guarantee that the feelings will be reciprocated by the children involved.

Because of the high divorce rate, second marriages are more frequent but often involve stepchildren and financial conflicts. Child support can test and add stress to a relationship as it places additional demands and financial strains on the marriage. This is especially true if the other parent of the children chooses to cause trouble. It is common for divorced couples to disagree over child support payments, visitation schedules and child rearing issues. These issues may be added to the normal difficulties in developing a relationship with a new partner.

On the other hand, it may also occur that a potential spouse with a child may bring pleasure and joy into a new marriage. The child may provide a new parenting experience to someone who wants to be part of a child's life and for some reason has not yet been able to fulfill this desire. It is also true that a someone who already has children may want to parent differently with a stepchild. This person may regret how he or she treated his or her own child and welcome the opportunity to act as a better parent with a stepchild.

This can also occur if both of the prospective marriage partners bring children into a second marriage. It is necessary to have a very adequate courtship period prior to marriage, which should give everyone a fairly accurate indication of how the families will mesh. As the weeks and months go by, with frequent contact, both marital prospects will be able to observe how well the children relate to and accept their new family. Here are some possible questions to explore:

- How do I relate to his or her young children? How does he or she relate to my young children?

- How do his or her teenagers get along with my teenagers?
- How does he or she act as parent to my infant or toddler? Does my child seem confused about who is Daddy or Mommy?
- How disruptive are the weekend visitations with his or her children?
- Under what conditions do I have to relate to his or her ex-spouse?
- Can we afford the child support payments?

The most important factor is the provision of ample opportunity to discuss and air negative reactions and to allow positive feelings to develop. Children may not reveal their feelings initially to a new stepparent or to new stepsiblings. Adults, as well, may be guarded and not willing to face their concerns as the two families attempt to blend.

Frank and Lily had much to discuss after Lily's children were introduced into their relationship.

Both Frank and Lily were divorced and had been single for many years. Frank and his wife had suffered through a stormy period after their three-year-old died from leukemia and a divorce followed soon after. Lily's husband had been verbally and physically abusive and their divorce occurred after a five-year marriage and two children.

By the time they met again at their high school reunion, Frank and Lily both were in their forties and were eager and ready to embark on a new relationship. They were surprised to discover that they lived only a few miles apart. Although they had never dated in high school, they enjoyed each other's company and had fun reminiscing about their former teachers and classmates.

Regular and frequent dinners, outings and movies followed. Frank was introduced to Lily's two children, eleven-year-old Flora and thirteen-year-old Tommy. Both were athletic and Frank looked forward to attending their soccer and basketball games. Since Frank was a sports enthusiast himself, he enjoyed coaching the children on weekends. Lily was delighted to see how well Frank related to her children. She observed how sensitive he was to their moods. He was never intrusive and always respected her authority. Furthermore, she could see that both Tommy and Flora seemed to welcome his presence.

After a few months of dating they became intimate and eagerly looked forward to their time together. Eventually marriage was discussed, but a major conflict surfaced: Frank explained that he had always wanted to raise a child of his own, but this desire had been thwarted by the unfortunate death of his only son. He hoped to see a child of his own grow to maturity.

However, Lily explained to Frank, "Look, I realize that I could have a third child and I would like to do it for you. But I can't. It was very stressful to me as a single mother raising these two children. I just don't feel able to start all over again even though it would be our child. I feel that I'm just now getting over the darkness and I can see a light at the end of the tunnel. Furthermore, there will be expensive years to come for the two I already have. As much as I love you, regretfully I just can't go though another pregnancy and raise a child at this point in my life."

Frank thought to himself: *I've received much joy from this new relationship, especially after so many disappointing dates and lonely years. Lily has provided me with love and companionship that I never expected to find. I'd better count my blessings and not ruin it.* He took a deep breath and replied slowly, "Lily, this is a difficult issue for me. We have found each other and this may be our last chance. However, I now realize that I will have to give up my hope of being a biological father and mourn the loss of my dream. I want to become a good father to your—or should I say our—children. Please allow me to think about this matter for a few days before making a final decision on starting our life together."

With tears in her eyes Lily hugged Frank and replied, "Of course I will."

The future for this couple looks positive. It illustrates one of the problems faced in many second marriages when there are children involved. "Trade-offs" are often necessary. If he decides to take the next step in his relationship with Lily, Frank's newfound love and his positive relationship with his prospective stepchildren will, hopefully, help compensate for the loss of his dream.

3. NO PREVIOUS MARRIAGE

A prospective partner having a previous marriage raises serious questions that do not exist when both marital prospects have a "clean slate." Such concerns can include:

- If there is a divorce (instead of a death), why did the divorce occur? Were there financial problems, addiction problems or sexual issues?
- Did either of the spousal partners in the previous marriage have a commitment problem or was it a poor match?
- Were any of the ten red flag items involved as a cause of the divorce?

Let's look at the relationship problems of Penny and Christopher.

Penny met Christopher on a blind date arranged by friends. Attracted to him, she knew he had been through a recent divorce and wondered what precipitated that breakup. On their first date she asked him. Christopher was very candid in answering her question: "It was my fault. I was having an affair with someone in my office and my ex-wife found out about it. Fortunately, we did not have children, so our divorce was not complicated."

In the discussion that followed, Christopher revealed, "You know, I hope I'm not like my father who cheated on my mother. They ended up in a very messy divorce when I was a teenager."

Penny was worried, even though it was only their first date. Christopher certainly seemed to be attractive and interesting, but she wondered, *Does it make sense for me to see him again if he calls? How do I know he will remain faithful to me? I haven't had a lot of dates recently and I would like to see him again. But is it wise? Why should I get so attached and involved when in the end I might get hurt?*

It is reasonable for Penny to have these doubts and we believe it will not be an easy decision for her to make. Because Penny has not had many recent dating opportunities, she may feel a sense of desperation. Penny yearns to have a romantic relationship. As a result, her judgment may be warped. However, Penny would be wise to consider very carefully whether Christopher has the capacity and qualities needed to sustain a long-term relationship.

The research is in conflict when we consider the odds of a happy marriage if one or both partners have been previously married. Dr. Kaman M. Heller presents an excellent article discussing this issue titled "Improving the Odds for Successful Second Marriages." Logically, unless the divorced person has his or her own serious emotional problems, the odds of success should be better the second time around.[10] But we suggest that you carefully consider our discussion concerning this checklist item.

4. SMALL AGE DIFFERENCE
Research on the subject of male-female age difference at the time of marriage is conflicting. Some authorities give an optimal age difference of two or three years with the male being the older partner. Others approve a difference up to fifteen years. David Biella presents an

interesting discussion on the topic in *Scientific American* titled "What is the best age difference for husband and wife?"[11] We believe when the age difference between spouses is under ten years, they most likely have similar historical and cultural experiences and backgrounds with music, movies, political events and folk heroes. Both will have lived during approximately the same generation and they are more likely to relate to and understand each other. Also, they are more likely to grow old together as compared with a couple who has a twenty-year age gap.

If there is a large age gap, each partner undergoes developmental changes differently. The wife may be of childbearing age while the husband is looking forward to retirement. Older spouse prospects may have children from former marriages with resulting substantial financial commitments. Health and vigor usually decline with age.

In considering older spouse seekers with a substantial age difference where such considerations are diminished—for example, if both male and female are in their fifties or beyond, with children grown and self-supporting—a twenty-year age difference may not be as significant. It may also be true if both parties are in reasonably good health. Age difference may not be a concern if both are more interested in companionship and in enjoying a supportive relationship than worried about the future and perhaps being left a widow or widower prematurely.

While there are some exceptions for the reasons mentioned, for the average spouse seeker there are many advantages if the age difference is small. Let's look at the case of Jed and Nellie, which illustrates how issues of health, money, retirement and life experiences may be significant.

Jed, age forty-five, met Nellie, age twenty-two, during a research project conducted by Jed, who was a professor of biology at the university from which Nellie was graduating shortly. They spent many hours together on the project and grew close.

About two weeks after graduation, Nellie was jogging one day in a nearby park and was surprised when she heard her name called. She turned and saw her former professor. Jed jogged along with her and suggested, "Hey, how about meeting me for dinner tonight?" Nellie was astonished and it showed. Jed went on, "Look, it's legal. You're not attending college anymore; you are a graduate." He laughed. Nellie also laughed, but she hesitated before answering. She took a good look at him and she noticed what a great body he had. He was wearing shorts and a tank top. She thought, *Hey, he looks a lot better now than he did in a white lab coat.*

So she agreed, "Sure, let's have dinner."

Dinner was great. They seemed to have similar interests and a lot to talk about. Nellie found out that Jed had never been married and wondered why. He seemed very eligible. If she had not known his actual age, she would have thought he was much younger, more like a guy in his twenties than someone in his forties. She found she really liked him and she knew the feeling was mutual.

After they dated for a few months, he invited her to his apartment and told her he was going to cook dinner. "You know," he said, "since I've never been married, I had to learn how to cook and now you will get a chance to grade me. I hope I pass."

Nellie, who had had several boyfriends, knew that the dinner probably was a prelude to something more intimate, but she accepted the invitation willingly and looked forward to the evening.

She knew that she wanted to have a family but thought that she would first like to get an advanced degree. Thus she would not have children until she was almost thirty and if she married someone Jed's age he would be a fifty-year-old father for their first child. She thought, *How far do I want to go with*

this very attractive guy? Does it make sense? He will be an older
father and husband if I continue with my goals. He seems to be in
good health, but what about twenty-five years from now?

Nellie did more mental arithmetic and realized that if she
married Jed, their first child would graduate high school with a
sixty-eight-year-old father. She also wondered whether Jed
would live to see a second or third child grow up. Would they
ever be grandparents together? Yet she decided, *I'm not going to*
worry about the future. I'll just go and enjoy the dinner. I'll learn
more about him and consider these problems later.

The doubts that Nellie considered make sense. With these
very real issues it would be wise for her to think further about
becoming involved and attached to Jed. She should realize that the
relationship could become more intense and much more difficult
to break off. Jed may also have ideas about a future family that differ
from Nellie's. If their relationship progresses, it would be advisable
for this couple to discuss these issues openly. Both should carefully
consider their backgrounds, present desires for a satisfying relationship and future plans.

5. SIMILAR EDUCATION
6. SIMILAR INTELLIGENCE

We are combining these two checklist items for discussion, because
there is a strong correlation between intelligence and education level.
Both evolutionary psychologist David Buss in *The Evolution of Desire*
and marriage and family therapy professor Jeffry Larson in *Should*
We Stay Together? agree that similarity of intelligence and educational
level increases the odds of marital satisfaction.[12] In the dating process
it is difficult to separate these two variables.

Similarity of intelligence between husband and wife "is critical
for successful mating," according to Buss.[13] A male with low average
intelligence probably has few similar interests with a female who

possesses a high IQ. Most high school dropouts have little in common with mates holding advanced academic degrees. Due to such educational and intellectual disparity, such mismatched partners may have little to share and enjoy together, despite a strong physical attraction. Yet each may have the capacity to form a happy union with someone else of similar intelligence and education.

If partners have similar education levels, they probably have much in common although their fields and degrees may be different. College and graduate degrees usually result in many and varied interests as well as more available career choices.

There are exceptions: a spouse prospect may have little formal education but may have superior intelligence, have a high degree of motivation and be very well self-educated.

Fortunately, the educational level of a prospective spouse should be easy to discover, even on the first or second date. Level of intelligence is somewhat more difficult to evaluate, but normal conversation covering a variety of topics during the dating period will give good insight. Overall, spouse seekers should do their best to remind themselves that physical/sexual attraction often challenges their ability to logically assess the capacity for intelligent interaction and wise behavior in a future mate.

Let's discuss Warren and Genevieve, a couple with very different backgrounds and intelligence levels.

Warren and Genevieve met at a faculty party when Warren was a professor at a major university. Warren had previously been a Rhodes Scholar at Oxford and had earned his Ph.D. before reaching age twenty-five. He was seen as a "comer" and was being groomed for tenure. Genevieve was a young receptionist and appointment clerk in the university's office of the dean. From the moment Warren laid eyes on her and danced with her at the faculty party, he was definitely smitten. Genevieve was a high school graduate, an excellent cook and had a great sense of style. She was also friendly, outgoing and a good listener. She had average intelligence and functioned well at her job.

Warren was proud to be associated with a glamorous woman and he delighted in showing her off at social functions to his academic friends and family. They married after a whirlwind six-week courtship. After an extended honeymoon, the couple returned to live close to the university campus and resumed their regular work schedules. Never before in Warren's life had he engaged in such regular and satisfying sex. He felt complete and content.

Since Warren was on the tenure track, he was expected to attend numerous faculty functions, such as teas, dinners, book signing parties, musicals, lectures, etc., which included considerable social interchange between those attending. Genevieve accompanied Warren to these functions. Other professors and their wives, all of whom were college graduates with advanced degrees, also came to the events. The wives were very friendly to Genevieve, but from the very beginning, she felt uncomfortable, as these professors and their wives discussed current events, political elections, the latest books or plays and various other academic and intellectual subjects. Genevieve had difficulty joining in any of these discussions. She read little and preferred magazines rather than books and enjoyed game and reality shows. Since she had no children and wasn't sure she was even ready to begin a family, she felt unable to discuss the stresses or joys of childrearing with the other women.

She tried to explain her discomfort to Warren, but he brushed it off and said, "Oh, don't worry. You can charm these gals. I know you can handle them." As time went on, Genevieve became aware that she and Warren actually had very little to talk about. Their physical relationship was great, but when they were alone together, either at home or elsewhere, Warren showed no interest in watching the soap operas and game shows Genevieve loved and instead immersed himself in working on his ongoing lectures or various publications in progress.

Warren and Genevieve are unable to fulfill the most essential of the four spousal roles discussed earlier: friend/companion/advisor. In view of the vast disparity between them in both education and intelligence levels, their relationship is unlikely to improve. Their long-term marital prospects are bleak. Successful marriage is dependent upon far more than sexual compatibility and requires a mutual feeling of friendship and companionship, which for this couple seems to be lacking.

Had this couple avoided their whirlwind courtship and the trap of marriage so soon after meeting, there would have been time and opportunity when each could have clearly determined that they had very little in common and were a poor match. This is the reason why a long courtship is essential.

7. SAME RACE, RELIGION AND CULTURE

Today, according to data from the Pew Research Center, "one in seven new marriages is between spouses of different races or ethnicities."[14] There is considerable conflict in the research on whether the odds of divorce are greater in an interracial, intercultural or interreligious marriage. According to the studies presented in "'But Will It Last?': Marital Instability Among Interracial and Same-Race Couples," authors Jenifer L. Bratter and Rosalind B. King state that although "overall, interracial couples have higher rates of divorce," the results can vary according to race and gender. For example, Bratter and King's studies indicate that marriages between black men and white women are twice as likely as white/white marriages to end in divorce. Similarly, interracial marriages among non-whites "experienced less marital stability than their same-race married coethnics."[15] But a marriage with a white husband and black wife is 44 percent less likely to end in divorce as compared to a white/white couple.

Conversely, social psychologists such as Donn Byrne and Sarah Murnen in "Maintaining Loving Relationships," who examined the literature discussing the role of race, religion and culture in connection with mate selection, still maintain that the odds for a successful partnership are increased when the partners come from similar races, religions and cultures. They conclude that similarity in these areas enhances marital happiness.[16]

The research on cultural, racial and religious intermarriage reveals that there are no simple answers and there is no doubt that this topic raises complex issues. It seems that no hard and fast rules can be made on the pros and cons of such marriages. We feel that race, religion and culture constitute only one of the many checklist factors that spouse seekers should consider. Overall, we agree with the psychologists who maintain that the odds for a successful partnership are increased when male and female come from similar races, religions and cultures. It seems logical that differing values, traditions and lifestyles can create tensions between partners.

Before making the decision to marry, it is important to explore these potential conflict areas and differences during a long courtship, because early dating experiences may not allow enough time for such problems to surface. The interracial relationship of Melanie and Marvin illustrates some possible potential areas of strength and conflict.

Melanie and Marvin met in a small informal study group while both were first-year law students. Marvin had joined the group when he was invited to sit in on a study session one evening by his friend, Arnold, who told him, "Look, there are four girls in this group. They want a male member and I don't want to go alone. Come on. See how you like it. These girls are super smart. I figured they might help me to learn this stuff. It could help you, too. What have you got to lose?" Marvin thought about it briefly. He had no other plans that evening and knew he wanted to join a study group anyway. "Okay, I'll go," he said, "but I may not actually join. I'll just look."

That evening he met the group. As they began to discuss the day's assigned topic, Marvin understood why Arnold was so interested in the group. They were all very bright and very prepared as they discussed a contract law problem. Marvin sat next to Melanie, one of the two young black women, and found her to be vivacious and very well prepared. At the end of their first session, he told the others, "I'm in if you'll have me." They all laughed agreeably. As they left, Marvin asked Melanie, "How about some coffee?" Melanie agreed.

By the end of that semester, Marvin and Melanie's romance had blossomed and they had even discussed marriage and a life together after law school. They made plans to meet each other's families.

Marvin was introduced to Melanie's relatives at her cousin's wedding. He was the only white person at the ceremony but rapidly forgot about being self-conscious when they welcomed and received him so cordially. Melanie was the only college graduate of her large, extensive black family and Marvin become aware of this difference as he spoke to the guests. Afterwards, Marvin and Melanie discussed the differences between Marvin's largely professional relatives and Melanie's blue collar ones. "How will these post office employees, department store clerks and cab drivers get along with my relatives—doctors, lawyers, engineers and business executives?"

Melanie laughed. "Look, sweetheart, you and I are the ones who will be getting married, not our families. I think it will all be okay."

Marvin also felt good about their families. He was particularly pleased to see Melanie was so well received by his parents and his sister when she visited his home during a school break. They included her as they discussed their future summer plans and told her how they hoped she would join them.

How will Melanie and Marvin fare if they marry? The couple appears well matched in education, but even assuming they have the capacity for long-term commitment and the support of both families, they still may experience major problems. Aside from the black-white issue is the disparity in social, educational and economic status of the families. The arrival of children may bring additional stresses. Although such a union will result in a "NO" check for item 7, such a marriage can work very well if the partners are otherwise well matched and are willing to explore and face the cultural pressures that may put stress on their marriage. Younger couples may find a society more supportive and accepting of mixed racial marriages. Yet for many couples, racial and cultural differences may still be an important issue to face and explore before marriage.

Jill and Bart are an interreligious couple who also must explore potential areas which may be problematic.

Jill and Bart met during their second year of an MBA program at a large university. By chance they happened to sit together during a crowded cafeteria lunch. Jill looked up into his blue eyes as he apologized for bumping into her chair and felt a strange surge of emotion as she said, "No problem. It's tough finding a vacant chair in this place."

"Thanks. I guess this is my lucky day," he replied as he put his tray down and slipped in next to her.

Bart couldn't keep his eyes on his food. He didn't want to stare at Jill, but she was a striking blonde beauty.

Neither Jill nor Bart had any classes until after three o'clock so they sat talking, not even noticing that the cafeteria cleared out and the other students left. Both found they were active in school politics, where there was a distinct conservative/liberal political battle raging. It was particularly intense, because all the students were of voting age and the presidential battle was in full swing. They found that both were liberal

Democrats and had signed up to distribute information about voting on Election Day.

"I can't understand why we never met," said Bart.

"Well," replied Jill, smiling, "better late than never, wouldn't you say?" And Jill really meant it. She felt their meeting was memorable and important. Bart was certainly different from her other male friends and she thought to herself, *This guy has possibilities.*

Bart told Jill that his parents were rock-ribbed Republicans whose political agenda closely tracked that of Rush Limbaugh. Jill was surprised. "So what was it that made you become a liberal Democrat? It certainly is the opposite of your mom and dad."

Bart agreed and said, "Well, maybe I just wanted to be an independent thinker. I guess I was also influenced by my freshman political science professor." They planned to meet later that evening for dinner as they shuffled off to class. While walking to class, Bart reflected, *I know this love at first sight business is nonsense, but it's hard to deny that I was impressed by her at lunch.*

After eating dinner together and seeing that they concurred on an amazing number of topics, Bart said to Jill, "Say, how about coming out on my family's boat this weekend? It's going to be nice and warm and I can teach you a little about sailing if you don't know anything about it." Jill agreed and asked where this would take place. Bart replied that his family had a thirty-five-foot powerboat at the local marina and that they would have the boat to themselves that particular weekend since his family was out of town and his two brothers were visiting friends in another city. Bart suggested, "Let's bring lunch and spend the day. We can go out in the bay and maybe into the ocean if it isn't too rough." Jill, who had been an avid canoeist and sailor all her life, agreed. The next few days they had lunch and dinner together and by the time the weekend arrived, both were eagerly looking forward to their day on the boat.

On Saturday morning, Jill and Bart met for breakfast at the local yacht club. Jill had never been there before and was impressed at the sheer luxury of the whole place. There was one large, expensive boat after another. When they arrived at his family's boat, she noticed that it was very luxurious and that Bart seemed to know exactly what to do. He quickly cast off and they sailed into the bay. It was a warm, sunny day and by midday there was not a cloud in the sky. Bart anchored the boat in a little inlet and they settled down for lunch. They sat close together and it was so hot that they stripped down to their bathing suits.

After eating, Bart suggested a swim. "Great," replied Jill. They both dove into the water and she could see that he was very coordinated and well proportioned. She also noticed he was an excellent swimmer as was she. They enjoyed swimming together back and forth across the small inlet. When they climbed back onboard, Bart jumped onto the transom and then pulled Jill up. As he did so, she slipped and fell against him. His arms went around her to keep her from falling. Before they knew it, they were wrapped in a warm embrace. Bart took her hand and they went below into the spacious cabin.

After a truly pleasurable sexual interlude, Bart said to Jill, "I've never felt like this before. I can't explain it." Jill smiled; she also had a very positive feeling about Bart.

Reluctantly they went back to the dock. Just before they said goodbye, Bart said, "Jill, we're having a dance at my parents' country club this Saturday night. I'd like to bring you and introduce you to my mother and father."

Jill said, "Okay, I'm glad to go. It should be fun. I bet I'll be the only Jewish girl there."

Bart seemed surprised. "Jewish?" he said. "I didn't know you were Jewish."

She asked, "Well, does that make a big difference to you?"

Bart smiled. "No, not to me," he replied. "My only problem is going to be keeping the other guys from taking you away from me. They've probably never seen such a beauty, whatever the religion." She smiled and they parted.

Dinner and dancing at the country club affair was fun and Jill was warmly received by Bart's parents. Nothing was said about her religion, yet she noticed that she appeared to be the only Jewish person present. At dinner there were some discussions about up-and-coming political candidates and it became clear that this was largely a conservative Republican crowd. She was not surprised since Bart had clued her in to their leanings.

In the weeks that followed, Bart and Jill remained very close and began to discuss marriage, even though Jill knew it was somewhat premature. Then one evening at dinner, the subject of religion came up and Jill mentioned to Bart that even though she was Jewish, she wasn't very religious and didn't believe that there was a God or a supreme being.

She told Bart, "I can't stomach much that is in traditional religion."

Bart was surprised. "I intend to tithe at least ten percent of my earnings to the Church."

"Tithe? What does that mean?" Jill inquired. Bart explained to her that this meant that he would dedicate at least ten percent of his earnings to Jesus Christ and the Church and he felt that this was the duty of every Christian. "Furthermore," he said, "I hope my children will be baptized into the Christian faith." He looked at her, waiting for her reaction.

Jill did not reply. She had not contemplated how different his religious beliefs were from her agnostic leanings. She kept these thoughts to herself.

If these two elect to marry, conflict over religion may be imminent. It is unlikely that either will change his or her basic beliefs about religion. The gulf between them may be too wide. Physical attraction and agreement on politics may sustain their relationship for a time, but the arrival of children and decisions about their religious upbringing will cause trouble because of these differing religious beliefs: Bart's tithing of ten percent of his earnings and Jill's lack of spiritual beliefs and religious commitment. Their future together will mostly likely be fraught with problems that will be very difficult to resolve.

This underscores the necessity of seriously considering partners' individual attitudes concerning religion. There are many interreligious marriages that work out very well, because the religious differences do not cause conflict between the partners. Despite the fact that husband and wife sincerely believe in the tenets of each of their respective religions, there may be no problem if they agree on how they will educate and expose their children to religion. For example, a Christian and Jewish couple might agree to raise their children without any specific religious affiliation, attending neither church nor synagogue, yet enjoy and celebrate the various holidays in both religions. There are many mixed marriages where this is done and there is neither stress nor conflict over the issue. With other couples, one of the partners may wish to convert and embrace the other's religion, feeling comfortable in that spiritual environment. The key question to be answered by couples contemplating such an intermixed marriage: Will our different religions, races or cultures cause conflict if we marry?

8. ADEQUATE OR POTENTIAL ASSETS/INCOME

Historically in most cultures, women, who bear the children, have looked to men to provide financial security for them and their children. In modern day society, some women, particularly those who want or plan to be stay-at-home mothers, need to determine during dating and courtship whether their prospective spouses can carry the financial burden.

- Does the prospective spouse either earn a reasonable income or have the education, motivation and potential to do so?
- Aside from income, do one or both partners possess other assets or non-financial advantages that may be helpful to the future marriage, such as inheritance, investments, unique abilities or talents?

In today's world, many women provide equal or greater income than their male partners. There are also numerous couples where female contributions help assure and sustain the financial security of the marriage. But financial queries are still important. Will there be enough money to sustain the expected lifestyle of the future family particularly when children arrive and if one parent wishes to stay home as the primary caregiver? Explore these questions during the courtship period, but remember we cannot predict economic events that may put stress on the marriage. In addition, psychologist David Buss explains the importance of gauging the future potential of a prospective spouse who may lack present resources but who exhibits the promise of future financial security. Other qualities in the person, (judgment, motivation, etc.) may predict how he or she will handle prospective financial issues.[17] College educated men and women know that their incomes will be augmented once they have graduated from their respective programs.

Once partners seriously consider marriage, we suggest they work together calculating projected income and expenses for the first months of marriage. As marital authority John Gottman suggests in *The Seven Principles for Making Marriage Work*, "clear-headed budgeting" is helpful.[18] Such joint financial discussions will also help couples determine how well they will function together in other areas of their future married lives. Let's look at a couple who had to consider the financial implications of certain career paths.

Ben and Debra met when both were acting in a university play. Both played important roles and thoroughly enjoyed the experience. They began dating and a serious romance soon blossomed.

Ben had so enjoyed his acting experience that he told Debra, "I have been preparing myself for a career as an English teacher, but this experience has made me think I might want to be a professional actor." Debra was surprised. She had pictured a much different future and although marriage had not yet been discussed, she had certainly dreamed about a possible life together with Ben involving both of them enjoying teaching careers in a suburban setting.

She replied, "I guess for you that means Broadway or Hollywood."

Ben replied, "Maybe so. I'd really like to follow my passion even though I realize it is hard to make a living as an actor."

Debra acknowledged that he did seem to be a gifted actor, but she also realized that her future fantasies of a predictable married life with a steady income might require serious alteration. She wondered, *Could I take the role of an actor's wife with many uncertainties about income, separations because of acting performances out of town and other stresses?* She thought carefully. *Maybe I should put our relationship on hold while I think about this.*

Debra decided to share her concerns with Ben. In the days that followed, Ben also began to have doubts about his acting career. He understood the many advantages of the stable and predictable teaching profession as contrasted with being a performer. After graduation, Ben became an English teacher and drama coach. On weekends and evenings, he participated in neighborhood theater productions, as both an actor and a director. He was happy and his relationship with Debra thrived!

Debra showed commendable maturity in her evaluation of her relationship with Ben. She recognized the financial and other problems created by such a career choice and that the amount of income earned would determine a future lifestyle: a house in the suburbs or an apartment in the city; the ability to act as a stay-at-home parent or the need to work full-time to pay the bills; a pension provided through teaching or unpredictable income from acting.

Luckily, Debra and Ben discussed this issue early in their relationship and had resolution not occurred, they could have separated if the career choice became an issue. It may be difficult to put a relationship on hold or break a relationship once an attachment becomes strong. A breakup can be even more difficult if there have been very satisfactory sexual relations and deep romantic feelings have developed. This again underscores the importance and desirability of an early evaluation of the prospective spouse before the attachment and bond is so developed that separation is difficult and painful. Much unhappiness might be avoided if the issues dealing with income and career choices are explored early in the courtship.

FAMILY HISTORY

The issues dealing with family history may be difficult to explore partially because they involve the preverbal as well as the early years of life. These items may bring up unpleasant memories and events that many do not wish to share or even face. For example, abuse by a parent or sibling may be painful to reveal, especially during the first few dates. Even in an extended courtship many partners may be reluctant to discuss these issues or cannot remember these events. However, as we have previously stated, the quality of early relationships is extremely important in the spouse selection process since they have long-range implications concerning the capacity to sustain a relationship. Therefore we encourage an exploration of the Family History items with a potential mate at appropriate times during the courtship.

*9. WELL TREATED, LOVED AND NURTURED IN EARLY YEARS

Attachment theorists examine the development of the quality of relationships from infancy onward. Psychiatrist John Bowlby developed attachment theory and explains that adult behavior is related to one's personal history. Early childhood experiences have profound influence upon later behavior, including children's experiences with attachments, separations and losses.[19] A child who feels loved and nurtured in the first years of life usually will, as an adult, have the capacity to transfer warmth and affection to those who are important: spouse, children, friends and others. In contrast, a child who has been neglected, mistreated, abandoned or abused may never develop the capacity to give or receive love.

The negative consequences of abuse in the early years cannot be overstated. Authors Ken Magid and Carole McKelvey explain this concept in their book *High Risk: Children without a Conscience.* They point out that children who are victims of early abuse are at risk of "never being able to experience the most important human emotion—love."[20] There are degrees of abuse, both physical and psychological, and we must not forget, as psychologist Judith Wallerstein points out, that some children are amazingly resilient and can become excellent spouses despite early negative experiences.[21]

It is crucial to carefully explore the early years of your prospective spouse, especially his or her first five years when critical attachments are formed. During this time a child learns to trust, discovers that he or she is lovable and valued and feels that it is safe to return this trust and love. Or it can be the time when a neglected or abused child learns that it is too painful to form close attachments and that intimacy and trust are too dangerous to risk. This coincides with our earlier discussion on those who cannot commit.

Later traumatic events can occur that may influence a person's capacity to form a committed relationship. However, an emotionally healthy foundation during the first five years of childhood can help mitigate the negative effects of such later trauma. Therefore, despite divorce, family deaths or serious illness during school age or adolescent years, a potential spouse still may have the capacity to develop positive long-term relationships if he or she was well treated, loved and nurtured in the early years of life.

Katie is an example of a young adult who had positive early experiences.

Katie was optimistic, curious, adventuresome, generous and trusting. When reminiscing about her childhood, she remembered her stable, predictable and loving family. Her parents performed their roles as father and mother admirably and Katie always felt she was the important center of her parents' lives.

Katie's parents often recalled that she was a captivating and vivacious young girl and they never tired of telling about the baby and toddler preschool years and her foibles during that time. Their enjoyment of her early years certainly was reflected in Katie's capacity to become a secure and loving spouse.

However, their family life also had its sorrows and problems. When Katie was ten, her younger brother Zack developed leukemia and died within a year. This tragedy deeply affected all members of Katie's family. During the last year of Zack's life, none of the siblings, including Katie, received much attention. The focus was understandably on Zack, who needed constant care, frequent visits to the doctor and expenditures for equipment and medicines, all of which put stress on Katie's parents.

In the year after Zack's death, her mom and dad were in mourning. Their grief hung like a dark cloud over the family. However, the early stable family structure created by Katie's mother and father provided Katie and her siblings with the emotional capacity to withstand the strain and tension and to deal with the sorrowful loss.

In later years when they talked about Zack, her parents reaffirmed how they had all pulled together through a difficult time. They also acknowledged how stressful Zack's illness had been to Katie and her siblings.

Because of her secure early years and the strong attachments and bonds with her parents and siblings, Katie was able to weather the stressful period of Zack's illness and death. Despite experiencing this family tragedy, Katie retained her capacity to develop into a kind, generous and mature adult with the ability to give and receive love.

10. SAME CAREGIVER(S) TO AGE THREE

Child development experts have found that very young children who experience continuity of care with loving parents and have few caregiver changes are more likely to form committed adult relationships. Especially over the last thirty years, many infants and toddlers have experienced "caregiver roulette" in which caregivers are constantly changed and the children never know in whose arms they will land. Such frequent changes of primary caregivers for preverbal children can have negative consequences.[22] Such "normative abuse," a term created by psychotherapist and author Karen Walant, could significantly interfere with the child's ability to trust and form secure attachments.[23]

The caregiver history of a potential spouse is important, because continuity and predictability of care for the very young are essential, either with a parent or a substitute caregiver. Disruptions of the attachment process can have a little-understood delayed effect that can significantly influence future relationships. It may be difficult to make the connection between an infant who is the victim of "caregiver roulette" and the same person thirty years later who has two failed marriages and can't seem to commit. But there is ample clinical evidence of a cause and effect relationship, which is illustrated in the case of Timmy.

During the first four months of his life, Timmy's mom and dad cared for him. They changed his diapers and responded quickly if he cried. He knew his mom's smell, voice and special way of holding him. Then his routine was abruptly shattered when his mother went back to work. A new caregiver took over and Timmy's life significantly changed. The continuity of care by his mother was altered and the bond that he had begun forging with his mother was still fragile and not solid. This was a very severe blow to Timmy's emotional stability. Unfortunately, Timmy was not able to speak and there was no way for Timmy's mother to prepare him for her abrupt departure or the introduction of another caregiver.

Despite the fact that Timmy lacked language, he, like other infants, was quite resilient. Eventually he learned to trust Betty, who was the first person who took over after his mother went back to work. Timmy was able to establish a positive bond with her. Gradually he learned to be comfortable with her. She was predictable and nurturing and she seemed able to meet his needs.

Then, four months later, the same thing happened as when his mother returned to work. Betty left abruptly, having to deal with a family tragedy, and a new primary caregiver, Agatha, took over. But after a few months, she also departed. Timmy was then about one year old. His parents started bringing him to spend the day at Jenny's house. To get there Timmy had to leave his familiar crib and his home early in the morning. In addition to Timmy, Jenny took care of another little baby and three other children. She was different from his mom, Betty or Agatha. She had a strange smell and a different voice.

Child psychologist and author Dr. Penelope Leach describes in her book *Children First: What Society Must Do—and is Not Doing—*

for Children Today the feeling of "despair" Timmy experienced when deserted by so many caregivers, both those with whom he had developed a bond or others who came and went. She explains how a baby feels deserted even though the desertion is "no more than a parent's routine of leaving for their job."[24] In the situation described, Timmy's problem was compounded by the fact that this abandonment happened repeatedly. He experienced "caregiver roulette" in the preverbal years. These separations were very stressful, because as an infant and toddler Timmy had no sense of time and no ability to be verbally prepared for the changes he had to face. He would have had a difficult time retaining the image of his mother in his mind so as to anticipate her return.

As an adult, Tim had difficulty in trusting a future spouse. As he described his feelings, Tim said, "I am reluctant to get close to others. I am concerned that my partner doesn't really love me or want to remain together with me. I yearn to depend on someone but they seem to run away."

He is actually restating the feelings he most likely had in his first years of life when he experienced so many changes in caregivers and never learned to trust that anyone would really be there for him. Despite the fact that the experience occurred many years before adulthood, these early feelings of mistrust and insecurity are real impediments to sustaining a successful relationship. There is a delayed effect, because early negative experiences may not manifest themselves until many years later.

Tim's story underscores the importance of investigating and carefully considering the very early years of a prospective spouse. This does not mean that you should automatically rule out a marital prospect who has a history similar to Tim. Recent research has shown that many such children are emotionally resilient and capable of becoming excellent lifetime partners if later in their lives they experience a reparative relationship or therapy that focuses on building trust and creating committed attachments.

As we've observed before, a sufficiently long engagement and careful observation will help a spouse seeker make a decision once he or she has had adequate opportunity to observe and learn about the early life of a prospective partner. Some questions you might pose to a potential mate: Can you remember who took care of you when you were little? Were your parents involved in your care? If no parents were involved, how many other persons were involved? Bring these types of questions up in normal conversations; no "third degree" atmosphere need be created.

11. PARENTS REMAINED MARRIED THROUGH TEEN YEARS

A possible future mate who comes from a broken home and whose parents are divorced, particularly if the divorce occurred sometime between infancy and adolescence, is a cause for concern. A child who experiences a stable nuclear family during his or her growing years may feel emotionally secure and will be better able to commit to and sustain a long-term relationship. On the other hand, if the nuclear family is disrupted by divorce, there may be a significant intergenerational effect upon a child since he or she will then often live through years of disruption and conflict. Journalist Caitlin Flanagan explores the family problems caused by divorce in her *Time* article "Is There Hope for the American Marriage?" She details how children can suffer from the collapse of their parents' marriage and the subsequent divorce.[25] Here are some major problems and jarring adjustments children of divorced parents face:

- Children may "learn" that conflicts are seldom peacefully resolved and that divorce is the answer. They may see that deciding to leave a marriage rather than working out solutions may be easier. Parents who walk away from conflict model for their children a lack of commitment to the relationship and to the institution of marriage.
- Familiar surroundings may disappear, because the family home may have to be sold so that the assets can be divided.

- Children may be shunted back and forth between the two new households of the divorced parents.
- Children may need to change schools, adjust to new neighborhoods and establish new sets of friends if the family is forced to move.
- Both parents and especially former stay-at-home mothers (or fathers) may be required to work or work longer hours, leaving children alone or in unsatisfactory care, since two households require more income.
- Children may have to cope with new parental substitutes. Often one or both parents must work and the father and mother may employ different babysitters. This is particularly difficult for pre-verbal infants and toddlers and may result in the previously discussed "caregiver roulette."
- Contact with grandparents may be less available if parents move to a new location. Grandparents are important, especially if they have sustained their own stable marriage. They can model for their grandchildren that it is possible to have a workable marital alliance. A grandparent can also act as a substitute parent if either mother or father is missing from the children's lives.
- Parents may begin to date and spend time with other adults, giving less time and attention to their own children.
- New rules, expectations and routines may be required, e.g., "Now you're the man of the house" or "Now you are mama's new partner and helper." These events may deprive children of carefree childhoods.
- Anger, frustration, sadness and despair may consume one or both parents, affecting their children.
- There is little time for laughter, loving words, relaxed and mellow outings and other joyful celebrations in the family home.

Partners sometimes choose divorce and other times divorce may be necessary if there is abuse, alcoholism, addiction or other extreme circumstances. We suggest that those seeking mates take a careful look at spouse prospects whose parents divorced when they were young and attempt to answer this question: Did these potentially stressful events affect the capacity of the future spouse to commit and to perform as a loving mate?

Again, spouse seekers should avoid any decision to "dump" a marital prospect just because he or she has divorced parents. Marriage authority Judith Wallerstein, along with other researchers, has found that many adults are quite capable of becoming excellent spouses despite earlier negative histories.

The story of Boris and Danielle brings to light how a whirlwind courtship and marriage may cause two people with very different needs and interests to either adjust or break apart.

Boris and Danielle met on a blind date. Their mutual chemistry was immediate and intense. They were married after a rapid eleven-week courtship and Danielle became pregnant after they were married only two months. The pregnancy was not planned; it was the result of frequent and unprotected sex during an idyllic weekend to celebrate their two-month anniversary. Their marital trouble began in the sixth month of Danielle's pregnancy when she told Boris, "I'm getting bigger and bigger and I think we should ease up on sex. It might hurt the baby." Boris agreed, but after a week of no sex he was jumpy and irritable. He told himself, *Grow up, Boris. You're going to be a daddy so get used to no sex for now.*

During the weeks of self-enforced celibacy as the couple prepared for the arrival of the baby, other problems surfaced, particularly about how their evenings and weekends would be spent. Although he was very bright, Boris rarely read anything except the sports pages; otherwise, he sat for endless hours watching basketball and other sports on the television. Danielle was the opposite: an avid reader, her TV watching concentrated on cable news. Neither Boris nor Danielle had realized that they had such different interests during their short courtship, which had focused on sex.

Although both were aware of these differences after marriage and during Danielle's pregnancy, their attention was distracted by the arrival of their daughter, Celeste. Danielle and Boris were delighted with her arrival and rapidly became immersed in the many chores and pleasures of caring for their infant. Both enjoyed Celeste's first birthday party and that evening, after a very satisfying sexual interlude, they had their first serious discussion.

"You know," Danielle told Boris, "we are not a good match. As smart as you are, you are still a sports jock. And I am exactly the opposite. Except for Celeste and the bedroom, we don't have much in common, do we?"

Boris was silent for a time, groping for his reply. "Yeah, I have been thinking the same thing for quite a while. It hasn't been much fun going to the games with the other guys and their wives; I'm always making excuses about why you're not with me. What do you think we should do? Should we call it quits like my mom and dad did when I was six years old?"

Danielle's reply was immediate: "Absolutely not! We made this choice and we should stick it out. We owe it to Celeste. So what if we are not such a great match? We should act like adults and think of Celeste. We can learn to accommodate. I'll even go to some of your games. And you can go with me to my book group now and then."

Boris smiled. "I knew when I met you that it was more than just your body. Yes, you are right. Let's just make up our minds and stick it out. Maybe someday things will work out." Boris pulled her closer as her eyes began to tear.

Boris and Danielle's conflicts and unhappy stoicism do not occur every time that couples arrive at the realization they are not well matched. However, many such couples divorce early in the marriage, creating the problems we have discussed for their children. But to this couple's credit, Boris and Danielle decided to put the interest of their baby daughter first and stay together through her childhood and adolescence. As an adult, Celeste will most likely bring to her future marriage emotional stability and the capacity to commit. It bodes well for her future family and subsequent generations.

*12. GOOD RELATIONS WITH PARENTS, SIBLINGS AND GRANDPARENTS

Much research reveals that the quality of a female's relationship with her father will strongly determine how she will deal with a partner of the opposite sex. In his book *Should We Stay Together?*, author, professor and therapist Jeffry Larson points out how critical and abusive treatment by a parent of a female teenager can create later difficulties as she attempts to relate to a prospective marriage partner.[26] Similarly, whether or not a male felt loved and nurtured by his mother will influence his attitudes toward his wife. It augurs well for any future union when the prospective spouses have had positive, loving and sustained relationships with their parents of the opposite sex. The same is true regarding an opposite sex sibling. Jennifer's poor relationships with both her father and brother point to later relationship problems.

Jennifer was just beginning to date seriously and search for a potential spouse. However, she was wary of becoming too close to Jim, her latest boyfriend. She was frightened when he became too excited or raised his voice and became upset at casual confrontations. She felt threatened when he disagreed with her even about minor issues.

When discussing her childhood with her therapist, she admitted hating her dad, who was rigid and punitive and had an explosive temper. Her older brother bullied her through her teenage years. Jennifer was apprehensive when relating to any male whose behavior at times reminded her of either her father or her older brother. Many of the negative feelings from her childhood were projected onto Jim, her potential future mate. Unless she gained some understanding about the cause of these feelings, there could be serious issues in relating to her male partner.

This same analysis applies to a male spouse prospect regarding his relationships with his mother, sister or even grandmother, who are the most important females in his early life. He would tend to be more loving and caring to a spouse if he experienced nurturing and responsive care from his mother and was close to his sister. However, even though studies indicate that such early family attachment patterns can influence later relationships in dealing with a spouse, such negative effects could be lessened by a positive relationship with a friend, therapist or counselor of the opposite sex. Also, therapy may help a person gain insight into how, as an adult, early family conflicts and stresses influenced negative attitudes and behavior toward a potential mate.

One important factor a prospective spouse may consider is how to find out whether or not a potential mate has any of these problems. During the early dating period, one might ask:

- Who was your favorite parent?
- Where did you go on holidays?
- How often do you see your brother(s)/sister(s)?

These questions could stimulate an informative discussion that will help a spouse seeker answer questions concerning the quality of the attachments within the family of a prospective partner.

We pointed out earlier how grandparents often play a significant role in the early life of a child. Many have acted as primary caregivers and as such can be a major influence on future attitudes and behaviors. When a secure attachment is formed between a grandparent and a child in the early years, it can help minimize the poor relationship between a child and his or her parent. Josie's story is an example of the pivotal role grandparents can have when parental relationships are weak.

Josie's parents divorced when she was three and a half years old. She had not yet had an opportunity to form a close bond with her father, who was away from home in his occupation as a national sales representative. She had no male siblings. Fortunately, she developed and maintained a very positive relationship with her grandfather, who operated a nearby hardware store.

During her early years, her grandfather and grandmother often cared for her while her mother was working. They also took her on many outings, including picnics, fairs and other community events. As a teenager, she enjoyed working in her grandfather's store selling to customers and stocking the shelves. She knew she was very important to her grandfather and she felt loved and appreciated.

Even though she had minimal contact with her biological father, her positive attachment to her grandfather promises a good prognosis for a future marriage.

Josie's example reveals how the lack of a positive relationship with the parent of the opposite sex can be repaired by developing a bond and attachment to another important male figure, such as a grandparent, brother or other relative.

Childhood abuse or severe neglect by one or both parents can have serious long-range effects. In addition to rape and heterosexual or homosexual abuse, children may be exposed to beatings, emotional rejection and repeated verbal abuse. To tell a child he is "no good," "worthless" or a "loser" may severely damage his self-esteem. If a parent threatens a child with abandonment or rejection, it can severely erode the child's relationship with that parent and in later years it may influence the person's attitudes toward a spouse of that same sex. Repeated name calling and threats can be as emotionally abusive as physical assaults. A child who is subjected to such treatment will often repeat the behavior toward his or her spouse or children at times of stress and conflict. A parent's voice and words may still be remembered.

Recall that this is a red flag item. A "NO" response will require very careful consideration if experience with the opposite sex parent or sibling was extremely negative. Careful inquiry is advisable to determine if such early traumas occurred, although we admit that such inquiry is not easy to accomplish.

13. OBSERVED AFFECTION BETWEEN PARENTS

Parents who display mutual affection are modeling loving behavior. Even if there is little overt hugging and kissing, a positive message may be communicated if mother and father have a harmonious "working alliance" without significant conflict or stress. However, if parents battle, never show affection or constantly belittle, nag and criticize each other, they are sending a negative message to their children. The unfortunate message is that it may be okay for a spouse prospect to repeat with a spouse the conduct he or she observed between his or her own mother and father. Or the prospective spouse may "learn" that it is permissible for a spouse to behave with hostility, to denigrate his or her partner and to withhold affection. In *Should We Stay Together?*, marriage and family therapist Jeffry Larson gives the example of a young man whose parents were involved in a bitter and highly conflicted marriage. Larson points out that this was a very poor model for their son in his own marriage.[27]

Ruth's family is an example of how affection between parents imparts a positive lesson.

Ruth recalled whenever her father came home from work at the end of a long day he always greeted her mother with a big hug. However, when he tried to kiss her she pushed him away and she said, "Not in front of the children." Nevertheless, Ruth could tell that her mother loved the affection. She often saw her mother reach out for her father's hand as they sat close to each other on the couch watching the news on TV.

Hopefully, your prospective spouse comes from a family that displayed positive behavior toward each other. But even if he or she grew up in a dysfunctional family where mother and father remained together despite problems, your future spouse still may have received a somewhat positive message: that the family as an institution was valued and sustained despite stress and hostility. The parents also provided a more stable and intact environment for their children and saved them from the trauma associated with divorce, despite conflict and stress in the home.

14. PARENTS: GOOD PHYSICAL/EMOTIONAL HEALTH, NO MAJOR ALCOHOL, DRUG OR OTHER PROBLEMS

As we've discussed, family problems, conflicts and stresses with which your prospective spouse was involved must be considered in the evaluation process. Therapist Larson describes how the mental illness or addiction of a parent can negatively affect children and create difficulties in their ability both to give and accept love. For example, if the mother or father of a future mate was addicted to alcohol or drugs, it is likely that as a young child he or she may have been exposed to abuse or neglect or was deprived of nurturing care. Children whose parents suffered major physical or psychological illnesses or early death may also be required to "grow up" too fast and may bring a residue of anger, anxiety and depression to a marriage. These children may have had to parent the parent and, as a result, missed out on their own childhoods. There may have been unexpected absences and prolonged separations that caused lasting apprehensiveness, fears and anger. These can cause lifelong negative effects on the children who are involved.

However, some children are quite resilient and are able to surmount such unfortunate past experiences and fulfill their roles as loving spouses. The time period when these traumatic experiences arose is also important. For example, a three-year-old may be more troubled by parental illness, hospitalization and consequent neglect as compared to a teenager who may be able to understand and cope with such problems.

Prolonged separation from a parent due to extended hospitalization can undermine a child's basic security and have long-range consequences. If your spouse prospect is saddled with such an unfortunate family history, careful inquiry as well as a long engagement should provide information to help you with your decision.

Edward's story reveals why it is so important to carefully investigate the early family history of a prospective spouse, in this case, the mental health of the mother.

At age five, Edward's mother suffered severe postpartum depression after the birth of Edward's younger brother Tommy. Unfortunately, their mother required extensive hospitalization and treatment extending over two years. As a five-year-old, Edward had very little understanding of the reasons for his mother's absence. He was left with anxiety and anger caused by the extended separation from his primary attachment figure. Even though he was told that his mother loved him and regretted their long separation, his anxiety and worries were not lessened.

As Edward matured, he performed very well academically. However, he remained fearful and cautious and was obsessed with staying close to home throughout his childhood, adolescence and even during his early adult years. At age twenty-eight, he met and courted Emily. She was two years his junior. Emily liked Edward, who was kind, intelligent and handsome. But she also noted he was very cautious and seemed curiously reluctant to join her for a weekend during which both were invited to a friend's wedding in a distant city. She asked him, "Edward, what's the problem? It'll be fun for both of us."

Edward replied, "I would really like to go and I agree that

it would be fun. But I must admit that it has always bothered me to travel out of our city and I have avoided traveling since I was a teenager. I even arranged to go to college in my home town."

Emily was concerned. She was very fond of Edward and she knew he felt the same way about her. Emily felt their relationship had definite long-term possibilities, but she wondered how such anxiety and fear might limit their life together.

Emily has good reason to be concerned. She will have to decide if she is willing to live with a husband who has this cluster of emotional problems. She might suggest to Edward that he seek professional help to overcome his fears and anxieties, but Edward may not agree with this. Or she could decide to end their relationship, despite her affection for him, because his neurotic behavior is too serious and disabling. But she knew that she had developed a strong attachment to Edward, who otherwise scored very well on the checklist with many positives. On balance, she decided that she would seriously consider remaining in the relationship and adjusting to his emotional disability.

The Edward/Emily story underscores the necessity of careful inquiry about the early life of a prospective spouse. It is also true that an average spouse seeker, like Emily, may not have seen the cause and effect relationship between the illness of Edward's mother when he was a child and his resulting long-term fears and anxieties that were apparent to Emily. Emily realized that it could be difficult to live with a person with Edward's background and problems. Every spouse seeker should be aware that early childhood experiences can influence adult behavior. This is why we have included the Family History section on our Prospective Spouse Checklist. Along with other information our book provides, this kind of awareness will definitely be helpful as spouse seekers make the important decision about whom they choose for lifetime partners.

PERSONALITY TRAITS/BEHAVIORS

All of the traits listed in items 15 through 25 tend to facilitate a harmonious relationship. However, it may be rare to find a spouse prospect who scores a "YES" on each one. Be aware that before marriage is the time to carefully consider such items. For example, many of us could accept a mate who is often late and disorganized if he or she has other important positive characteristics. You may even accept a mate who is gloomy and depressed if he or she is also kind, generous and considerate. Others may be willing to accept a mate despite the fact that he or she is stubborn and unwilling to accept advice if, otherwise, he or she is intelligent, stimulating and cheerful. Even lack of mature judgment is not necessarily fatal to a relationship if it is counterbalanced by sufficient positive qualities.

We suggest that you carefully explore and face each of these eleven personality factors and weigh their relative importance to you. There is enormous variation in spouse seekers' individual abilities and willingness to accept or reject the negative qualities in another person who is a candidate for a lifetime mate. In addition, all of us have the capacity to change over time, although it can be risky to count on any major modification of extreme behaviors.

15. KIND AND CONSIDERATE

A person who is kind and considerate usually has the capacity to be empathetic and responsive. These are important qualities in a potential mate, since they help to sustain the relationship and are much related to the ability to nurture and to give love and affection. In his book *The 6 Secrets of a Lasting Relationship*, psychiatrist Mark Goulston discusses how kindness and consideration for the spouse enhances marital satisfaction. He explains that in love relationships, it is "better to give than receive" and suggests you consider, "What does my partner want and need?" He also quotes Shakespeare, who said, "Love sought is good, but given unsought is better."[28] Spouses who are kind and considerate are often willing to care for and anticipate the needs of the other. This sustains and strengthens the husband/wife bond. A person who can go more than "halfway" and who is not upset if he or she gives more than he or she receives is a good candidate for a stable marriage.

On the other hand, while a person who withholds affection, time, money or consideration may still be intelligent, amusing and wealthy, etc., in the end he or she may be a marital risk.

As we have previously discussed, these behaviors usually come from the quality of a person's first attachments and are learned from responsive parenting in the early years. Facing and exploring such limitations in a potential mate may be important when deciding if you can live with someone who lacks the ability to show affection or withholds time or money. According to evolutionary biologist David Buss, kindness signals the willingness of a potential mate to commit energy and resources selflessly to a partner.[29]

The relationship of Fred and Andrea reveals how kindness even toward pets can give an important signal.

Fred was a thirty-two-year-old history professor with full tenure at a major university. He was very wealthy, having inherited a large fortune from his maternal grandfather. He was also physically attractive and exuded charm. He met Andrea at a faculty function. They had been dating for several months and he was very attracted to her. Their strong mutual physical attraction culminated in very satisfying sex.

However, Andrea felt uncomfortable when Fred began criticizing her clothes and even her cooking when she invited him to her apartment for dinner. She was surprised when he criticized the food she'd prepared and that he expressed no appreciation for all of her effort to create a romantic evening. Nor did he attempt to help in the after-dinner cleanup. Then Andrea noticed that Fred seemed to enjoy tormenting her beloved pet golden retriever. Andrea had hoped that Fred might be a serious marital prospect, but she began to question whether she could live with a husband who seemed unable or unwilling to display kindness, consideration or empathy regardless of his other attractive qualities.

Andrea was wise in raising and considering these disturbing questions and she should be very cautious about continuing with the relationship. If she does elect to continue seeing Fred, she should consider carefully whether Fred will, in time, reveal that he does have the capacity to be kind, considerate and empathetic. Although risky, perhaps she might suggest that Fred seek professional help.

It is essential that any potential partner possess these qualities or take steps to acquire them, since they form the foundation of a harmonious and loving relationship.

16. SENSE OF HUMOR

Laughter and humor can be quite therapeutic. In fact, some authorities contend that laughter can even help the immune system to fight and avoid disease. Whether or not this is true, there is no doubt that it is easier to live with humor as compared to someone who complains, whines and acts depressed. However, humor can be sarcastic or irritating. And, like any other characteristic, an excess of inappropriate humor may be quite annoying. Hopefully, your prospective spouse will provide your marriage with a pleasant balance of compatible fun and laughter as well as sober and serious conversation. Shared history, family experiences and similar educations can also create fertile soil for humor. Psychiatrist Mark Goulston explains the value of a sense of humor in marriage. He points out that "humor is a wonderful—and highly cost-effective—form of giving."[30] Life deals all of us many "downs" as well as "ups." It helps to find some humor in the rough events that we all inevitably face and you are indeed fortunate if your potential mate possesses the gift of humor.

The importance of humor can be seen in the relationship of Joanne and Jeff.

Joanne and Jeff were engaged to be married and they were living together before their anticipated July wedding. Joanne loved many qualities that Jeff possessed, but what she most appreciated was Jeff's humor. He was the wit of any gathering and she was amazed by his ability to remember amusing events, stories and jokes in detail and relate them so efficiently. Their courtship and the experience of living together were filled with fun because of Jeff's ability to deflect tension between the two of them when they argued. During their confrontations or disagreements, he often said something humorous and they both dissolved in laughter, making resolution of the conflict much easier. Joanne's only worry was that Jeff would quietly crack a joke at the altar and she would start to giggle uncontrollably.

17. CHEERFUL

Cheerful persons are optimistic, have positive expectations and have intrinsic faith that the future holds promise. A cheerful spouse may bring sunlight into the marital relationship, as contrasted with someone who sees doom and gloom lurking around every corner. Previously we discussed the impact of early events on a child's development. Such experiences in infancy and the preverbal years often determine whether a person is cheerful or depressed when an adult. When an infant's needs are responded to in a timely manner, the infant perceives the world in a positive light. When the child cries in distress and someone is always there to ease the discomfort, over time he or she develops a sense of optimism and feels "Good things will happen to me." Even though we are also born with temperamental differences, we learn to look at life influenced by our earliest experiences in the first years of life.[31]

There are occasional events such as death, illness and other losses that understandably cause sadness and despair. But such events are much different from chronic depression or a consistently gloomy and negative outlook on life, which can be created by repeated child neglect or abuse in the early years.

It may be difficult during casual dating to decide if a partner is basically cheerful or depressed. Over time it is essential to become aware of extreme mood swings. You will need to determine whether his or her emotional state and approach to life is one that you will find compatible in the years to come. If, during your own childhood, you lived with a depressed parent, your partner's negative disposition may not be so difficult to endure. Again, time during dating and courtship will help determine if this negative factor could be a serious issue in the future.

Delia and Lucas's story sheds light on evaluating this issue.

Delia was an attractive young woman and had her pick of boyfriends. She was unusually pretty and a talented dancer. She met Lucas, a management consultant, at a friend's potluck dinner and a warm and intimate relationship developed. However, Lucas noticed that Delia often seemed moody and sad. He asked her, "What's the trouble? We are great together, so why are you so blue? You have so much going for you."

Delia replied, "That is why I'm seeing a therapist. I couldn't make sense of my moods. But I have come to understand that some unfortunate early events that occurred in my life are affecting me now. My father left when I was a toddler. My mother had to leave every day for work. Different relatives took care of me. These experiences have left me with a pervasive feeling of sadness. I have learned that other sudden changes over which I had no control also contributed to a sense of gloom on my part. In time, with the help of my therapist, I believe that I will feel more positive about life and not feel so overwhelmed by my negative and depressed moods."

Lucas was encouraged that Delia was addressing this problem and felt that their relationship could continue with positive prospects.

Lucas did not have to investigate the circumstances of Delia's early life; she made it easy for him by her open and forthright discussion of her childhood and her ongoing therapy. This knowledge placed Lucas in a much better position to understand the basis of Delia's emotional states and mood swings. With the insight into the root of Delia's depression, he is in a better position to decide whether or not to stay in the relationship.

The arrival of a child and the stresses of parenthood can activate the symptoms of depression and bring a dramatic increase in any existing mental illness. Unfortunately, the emotional impact of childbirth cannot be determined during the dating and courtship period, although early history may provide clues about general emotional stability.

18. HAS FRIENDS

The ability to sustain and enjoy friendships indicates that the person has the capacity to form attachments and maintain them. It is similar to the commitment requirement, which we discussed earlier in this chapter. The number of friends is less significant as compared with the ability to form and maintain such relationships.

However, if a spouse prospect appears to have no friends outside the family or is a "loner" with few friends, this is an indication that the person may either consistently irritate others or that he or she is shy and afraid to socialize. Others may form friendships that do not last, because they cannot work through and survive minor hurts or insults. They may be wounded easily and break off contact abruptly. They may not have the ability to resolve conflicts or adjust to disappointments.

You may meet someone who has very few friends but is attractive, empathetic and very compatible. His or her relationships may seem quite shallow (i.e., many acquaintances, but no intimate friends). You may find it difficult to understand why she or he appears to have no relationships with any real depth outside of immediate family and relatives.

The answer may be that this person lacks the emotional energy or desire to relate to more than a few persons. But he or she may prove to be an excellent candidate to fulfill the four marital roles, so keep an open mind. Several months of dating should give the answer to these basic questions: Will this person be a satisfactory spouse despite such lack of social involvement? Does the potential mate have the capacity to sustain a relationship despite the fact that he or she has few or no friends?

Let's look at Ginny's experience with Ron to see an example of a relationship in which one person seems a loner but is actually a socially adept individual.

Ginny was very enthralled with Ron. He was a writer and was intelligent, creative and refreshingly different from her past boyfriends. Their chemistry was mutual and enjoyable. But Ginny noticed that Ron never made social plans and did not seem to have any close male or female relationships. She wondered why and thought, *Maybe because he comes from a large family with four brothers and sisters he never felt he needed friends.* His life seemed peppered with family obligations. But she also noticed that despite Ron's lack of friends, he seemed very comfortable with her own siblings and parents, all of whom responded positively to him.

Ginny had to admit that even though he seldom made plans on his own he seemed to enjoy her social contacts. He seemed interested in listening to tidbits of gossip and the problems her girlfriends faced. At times he offered to help or gave advice to her friends on investments or financial matters if they happened to be socializing together. Her friends found him congenial and seemed to have no problems relating to him. In fact, he was often the center of their discussions.

Ron's story demonstrates how the seemingly negative factor of few friends can be misleading. Ron is a very good example of someone who turned out to be an excellent spouse prospect despite his seemingly antisocial trait of having so few intimate relationships outside the family.

19. MATURE JUDGMENT

Life requires all of us to make many decisions on a wide range of issues. Some of these decisions, such as spouse selection, career choice, where to live and other aspects of lifestyle, are of great import and have long-term consequences. Other decisions, like what clothes to wear for a special occasion or what to order at a restaurant, are minor ones.

It is desirable to choose a mate who possesses the wisdom to think and act rationally and make prudent decisions. It is also true that a person can have good judgment in one area but act impulsively and immaturely in others. A wife can make level-headed decisions on childrearing issues but act irrationally when shopping for herself or for the home. But if the spouse prospect is inclined to be consistently impulsive and prone to act hastily, it may be an indication of future trouble and tension in the marital years. On the other hand, such negative behavior may be somewhat mitigated if there are other personality qualities that balance the relationship. His or her poor judgment may be neutralized by being able to accept his or her partner's cautions and flexible enough to change. As with many of the other items on the checklist, take the time to make observations and decide if you are willing to accept him or her even if there is a "NO" on this item. We also remind those using the checklist that evaluation of mature judgment is quite subjective and what could appear to be a rash and foolish decision for one may seem reasonable and prudent to another.

The story of David and Beth illustrates why a period of observation when judging a prospective spouse's decision making style is important.

David and Beth met while working in the administration office at a local hospital. They began to date and enjoyed being together. Beth thought that David might be a potential mate. They were strolling in a local mall one day and Beth saw David's eyes light up as they looked at an attractive promotional display of a beautiful red motorcycle.

A salesman, noticing their interest, approached them and said, "It's a sweetheart, isn't it? And it has a comfortable seat for your passenger." He smiled at Beth.

"I have a car," David said, "but to tell you the truth, I've always wanted a motorbike like this. But it's probably too expensive for me."

Still smiling, the salesman replied, "We realize that most people already have cars and are not going to switch all their transportation to a motorcycle. So we've got a very attractive package and we believe almost anyone can handle it financially. Let's go into my office and I'll show you some figures and explain." The salesman looked expectantly at the couple and began to walk toward his office, motioning to them to follow.

Beth shook her head and said to David, "Let's go on. Looking is fun, but it's not realistic. This would be a very big indulgence that we just don't need."

David, still thinking about the motorcycle, said, "I didn't plan to buy a motorbike, but what do we have to lose by listening to this salesman and getting an idea of what it would cost?" Beth was surprised, but she could see that David had been instantly captivated and intrigued by the idea. She decided to withhold her objection until the figures were presented. She was also interested to see how David would handle the situation, because she felt it would provide her with a good opportunity to see how he made decisions on expensive items.

In the office they listened to the salesman as he explained the deal, pointing out that there would be only a small down payment: "only two thousand dollars." Then he explained the payments would last "only six years at a low interest rate." Beth quickly calculated the cost including the initial deposit and found the total price with interest was well over nine thousand dollars. She felt that that figure alone would wane David's enthusiasm, but she waited, saying nothing but thinking, *I'll keep quiet. I want to see how David handles this.*

David sat silently for a time. Then he said to the salesmen, "You know, I could handle this, but as I think about it, I ask myself, should I? I have been regularly adding to my 401(k) plan and I'd have to stop it or certainly cut it down to put money into this motorcycle deal instead. And although I've always wanted such a motorbike, I think I'd better say, reluctantly, no thanks, and I certainly regret having to do so. But I do appreciate your time and wish you well with future customers."

Beth and David got up and walked out, hand in hand. Beth was relieved and excited. She told David, "I'm proud of your decision and the good judgment you just displayed. I know it wasn't easy."

With confidence, Beth can check "YES" on item 19 and be reassured that David, at least in this situation, showed that he has sound and mature judgment. Even though he really longed to own the object of his youthful dream, he listened and carefully weighed the pros and cons of spending his hard-earned money on this grown-up toy.

20. FLEXIBLE

Flexibility is, in part, related to the ability to be reasonable, empathetic and open to change. To be able to alter your thinking or behavior to accommodate someone else or to see another point of view is a valuable asset. This is especially true when two people live together. Jeffry Larson stresses the importance of flexibility in a marriage in *Should We Stay Together?* It is very difficult to sustain a marriage if either husband or wife is unbending, rigid and consistently demands his or her way.[32] An inflexible partner may obsess over his or her routines, diets, religious practices or political opinions. Examples might be a wife who refuses to accompany her husband to a ball game or a husband who refuses to join his spouse on a vacation out of the country or to see one of her "chick flicks." These acts of rigidity may seem minor, but they may be indicative of conduct that will put unnecessary stress on the relationship. Also, such rigid and inflexible thinking could become a problem when more serious topics are considered, such as having a child, what religion to raise the children in or a major move to another city. As life events occur, it is valuable and perhaps essential to have the capacity to show flexibility, to be able to modify attitudes and beliefs and to be responsive to another point of view. For example, changing one's diet or other lifestyle behaviors may be essential if one has a heart attack; refusal to do so could be serious.

While flexible behavior is important for a successful relationship, it is also true that partners may be able to live together quite satisfactorily despite rigidity on the part of one or both partners in certain areas. Time together, observation and experience during a long courtship and engagement will provide the opportunity to carefully consider this question before marriage. Some humor may also help in coping with each other's rigid or inflexible behavior.

Let's focus on one couple, Paul and Irene, who coped with their different tastes.

Paul and Irene were seriously considering marriage despite the differences in their interests and hobbies. Overall, they felt a strong affection and respect for each other and enjoyed being together. However, Irene was worried about their different interests and whether they might cause conflict over the years. One constant irritant was their different tastes in motion pictures. She liked foreign films with romantic themes, but Paul was a James Bond/Rambo enthusiast and these films were of no interest to Irene.

Irene decided to discuss the potential conflict with Paul, telling him, "Paul, I don't enjoy our regular battles over movies, yet I don't want to go to the movies alone. I want you with me and I don't want you to go by yourself to your movies either. I want to be together with you. But what can we do to handle this?" She looked at Paul expectantly.

Paul hesitated, thinking. Then, slowly he said, "You know, I'm glad you brought this up, because I have also been concerned. I don't like bickering about movies any more than you do and I have an idea for a permanent workable solution."

"Really? What is it?" Irene asked.

"It's simple," Paul replied. "I'll go with you to your picks and you go with me to movies that I select. In other words, we'll take turns. Who knows, I might even enjoy some of your movies one day." Irene smiled in agreement and hugged him appreciatively. She was pleased that she had brought up the subject for discussion.

This is a realistic example of a couple employing flexible behavior that augurs well for marriage. While movies might seem to be a very minor irritation for a couple, there are many such minor areas of conflict which, when added up, can cause stress. Irene and Paul were able to resolve their movie-going issues, because both were flexible and empathetic and in the end wanted to please each other. They will probably be able to translate this ability and the way they dealt with this issue to other areas of conflict in their life together.

21. PROMPT

We all know people who are consistently late and they always have an excuse. Such constant irritating behavior can cause anger, annoyance and insecurity. It can undermine any relationship. A spouse who is repeatedly kept waiting cannot help but feel devalued and angry, despite verbal protestations to the contrary. Some people have trouble making transitions; they may be reluctant to leave an activity or an appointment or to say good-bye. If, after considerable dating and courtship, your prospective spouse persists in this behavior pattern, you should ask yourself: Can I live with this annoyance for many years of marriage? Can I change my expectation that he or she will be on time? Can I accept such negative behavior in light of all the other positive qualities that he or she exhibits?

Terry and Alma are a couple who had to cope with one partner's irritating behavior.

Terry had proposed marriage to Alma and she happily said yes. They were both in sales and had known each other in high school, although they did not date until they re-met at a friend's wedding ten years later. Alma accepted Terry's proposal despite her knowledge that Terry had a very annoying habit: He was always late to every appointment, whether it was a dinner date, a doctor's visit or a movie. He often missed his flights as he delayed his departure from home and "unfortunately ran into traffic on the way to the airport."

Alma was really concerned about this problem behavior, because as a child her parents had taught her the value of promptness. Her mother impressed upon her "how disrespectful it is to keep people waiting." She was scolded if and when she was tardy. But Alma decided that she was willing to live with Terry's annoying behavior. Her reasoning was that she loved Terry very deeply and knew that it was reciprocated. She said to herself, *I'll never find another guy like him. He is handsome, smart, kind and generous. We have a lot in common.*

This is an excellent example of good reasoning by one partner to accept a spouse despite a very annoying trait: chronic tardiness. Alma felt that she could learn to live with and accept Terry as he was and she approached their wedding with her eyes "wide open." She was aware of the problem and was realistic about accepting it.

22. ORGANIZED AND NEAT

It can be very hard to live with a mate who is either excessively sloppy or compulsively neat. Both of these extremes cause much marital discord. What if your spouse prospect strews his or her clothes, papers and personal effects all over? You may not realize this problem exists until you either live with a prospective spouse or possibly spend extensive periods of time together (e.g., vacations). If both partners are neat and organized or if both are messy and casual with their papers and belongings, there may be little conflict. The basic question to consider is: How will it impact your future marital relationship? If, after an extended period of dating and courtship and (perhaps) living together, a lack of neatness or order is not a problem, a "NO" response for this item should not sound a marital alarm. But if there is stress in the relationship because of this issue, what can the couple do? Behavior modification with or without professional help may be useful, although this can be difficult and expensive. Both prospective marital partners should ask themselves this question before they commit: Will I be willing to tolerate such irritating conduct year after year? Some can. Some cannot.

One solution may be to hire a person to help with household chores so that, once or twice a month or even more often, the home is put in order. For some couples this may provide some relief from conflict over disorder and mess. The added expense is a better solution than separating from an excellent marital prospect or going through a divorce.

Roger and Natalie are a couple who chose to deal with the problem of messiness.

Roger and Natalie decided to get married but agreed that beforehand they would live together for a while, "just to make sure." Both Natalie and Roger felt it was a good way to determine if they would be compatible when they were together most of the time.

Problems surfaced as soon as they began living together. Both held full-time jobs and when they went to bed at night, Natalie noticed that Roger dumped his underwear and socks on the floor, along with anything else that did not absolutely have to be hung up. When Natalie rose in the morning to fix breakfast, she noticed that he left his possessions from the previous evening not only on the floor, but also on any other empty surface that seemed to be handy. Letters, notes, bills, newspapers and magazines were left in the bathroom, on the kitchen table, on counters and on the tops of bureaus.

Natalie found herself very irritated and upset. She said to herself, *I don't want to act like a nag, but I can't handle this. I'd better speak with Roger. We can't go on like this.*

One evening as they were eating dinner, Natalie took a deep breath and spoke in the friendliest voice she could muster. "Roger, we've never quarreled and we're getting married. I'm very happy that I found you and that you found me. But we have a problem."

"Problem? What problem?" asked Roger. "What could it possibly be? We are a perfect team."

"You just don't put any of your things away," answered Natalie. "When you go to bed at night, your dirty socks and underwear and anything else you don't need are left on the floor and you don't pick them up in the morning. Your mail is in the living room, bedroom and even in the bathroom. Things just stay wherever you've dropped them unless I put them in the laundry or their proper places."

Roger could see she was very irritated and he said, "I'm upset that you're upset. I guess I never learned to organize my things like you do. I've noticed that you're very neat and very well disciplined and I'm glad you told me. After all, I can't expect you to pick up after me like my mother or our house-keeper did. I realize it won't be easy and I'll need some reminders from you, but I promise you that our relationship is very important to me and since it bothers you, I am determined to change. I'll become more orderly and respect your sense of order. I will probably need you to nag me a little. Up to now no one expected me to be neat and organized. Maybe every now and then we can schedule a cleanup time."

Roger took a very constructive step by acknowledging the problem and promising to modify his behavior. It will probably not be easy for him to do this, but as he and Natalie live together for the next weeks or months before marriage, Natalie will have an opportunity to see if he actually carries out his promise. It may not be possible for Roger to significantly change his behavior. Natalie may have to determine if she can tolerate his messiness and control her annoyance and irritation in the years to come. Remember the decision to marry is not final until the "knot is tied."

*23. ABLE TO CONTROL ANGER

Abusive behavior, either physical or verbal, by one of the partners in a relationship is a frequent cause of divorce. If either prospective husband or wife flies into frequent rages and seems unable to control his or her anger, such behavior will inevitably place stress upon and disrupt the marital relationship, particularly if physical violence or verbal abuse is involved. Rage and explosive reaction can be frightening even to the abusers themselves. It also can generate anger in the recipient, who is the victim of such uncontrolled outbursts or inappropriate behavior. Rage responses often escalate into major conflicts between partners. It is important to examine the events that seem to precipitate these outbursts during the courtship and dating period. Frequent job changes may be an indication that a person has difficulty controlling anger; so may the loss of friends or the severing of family ties.

Important questions to explore: How does your future partner handle traffic jams, long lines, disagreements and disappointments? Is the angry reaction extreme or is it appropriate and understandable? Does he or she have a short fuse, take quick offense or feel easily hurt or injured? An excessive use of alcohol or other drugs may dissolve or inhibit normal self-control and precipitate such conduct.

It may be promising if a spouse prospect acknowledges that he or she has a problem with controlling anger and reacting to negative feelings. It is also encouraging if he or she seems to be willing to take proactive steps such as attending therapy or counseling to deal with this issue, but a "NO" should still be recorded for this checklist item. As with other red flag items, spouse seekers seriously need to consider this problem, because it is dangerous to ignore.

Donnie and Althea are a couple who contended with the serious problem of Donnie's anger episodes.

Donnie and Althea were both physical therapists working at different rehabilitation centers and had been dating for three months. Their physical attraction was strong and they seemed to have many common interests. Althea felt that Donnie had real spouse possibilities, with one important exception: When they disagreed, even over minor issues like what restaurant to choose, he sometimes reacted by cursing, yelling and flying into a rage. She could not understand how disagreements over minor decisions should upset him so. At dinner at one restaurant he threw a plate of pasta on the floor, because it was delivered cold. Then a short while after this he became so angry over a minor tiff, he shoved Althea against a wall. He apologized afterward, but Althea was very shaken by the event. She wondered, *Is this a serious problem and how should I handle it?*

Althea is certainly justified in her concern. Even though she still felt physically attracted to Donnie, she was upset about the implications of his anger episodes. Even if Donnie agrees to obtain help for his violent reactions, this inability to control anger will remain as a serious red flag item. There is no guarantee that therapy will be successful and that he will develop the tools to control his rages. Althea should first wait and see what therapy will accomplish before she makes any serious decision whether or not she should continue the relationship and marry Donnie.

If a couple plans to have a family and one partner has a serious anger issue, this is of major importance. Uncontrolled anger poses a real threat to both the spouse and the children. Children can become traumatized when exposed to parental rages and outbursts. Not only are they much smaller than the angry adult, but they are also powerless in the situation, since they are so dependent on the adult to care for and nurture them. They are emotionally trapped between experiencing fear and anxiety and feeling totally dependent and bonded to their mother or father.

One explanation for an inability to control anger stems from a person having suffered early abuse in his or her childhood. This may include extreme punishment and harsh discipline, which causes a child to feel powerless and impotent. In adulthood, when frustrated or confronted, similar feelings of impotence can emerge, causing the eruption of rage and anger. There is ample research dealing with the intergenerational effect of early child abuse on later expression of anger and rage. As psychiatrist John Bowlby explains in *The Making and Breaking of Affectional Bonds*, "each of us is apt to do unto others as we *have been* done by." (italics added)[33] As a result, we tend to repeat the pattern of nurturing or of abuse we experienced in childhood.

It is important to explore this issue during courtship by asking a potential spouse questions such as: Do you remember ever getting severely punished when you were young? Were you ever frightened of your mom or dad? Who was the one who usually got angry in your family? Did your mother or father ever become physically abusive with each other, you or your siblings? Did either of them act out while drinking or sober?

24. WILLING TO ACCEPT ADVICE

Most married couples are required to deal with decisions and choices ranging from the mundane—what tie or dress to wear to a dinner party or where to vacation—to the more substantial—whether or not to take a job offer in a different location or whether to have a child or another child. Such serious matters usually require extensive discussion and advice. This process can produce conflict, unless there is a mutual willingness to listen, consider and discuss the pros and cons. Those who are able to do so diplomatically and to both give and accept advice will have a closer and more compatible relationship. But partners who regularly argue, who seem incapable of listening to each other and who cannot seem to compromise will have problems when they marry. The willingness to listen and allow for "give and take" is essential to any well-functioning marriage. The ability to listen, consider and act on advice is related to other items on the checklist, such as Flexible, Kind and Considerate and Mature Judgment. Alex and June's story illustrates how advice might be offered, received and ultimately acted upon.

Alex, a baseball coach, experienced considerable back pain. He and June had been dating for some time and he mentioned to her he had visited his doctor and after several tests his doctor had suggested that he have immediate back surgery. June, even though she was a registered nurse at a local hospital, was reluctant to give medical advice, but in this case she felt she should speak up. She advised Alex that in her opinion, before any serious surgery should occur, he should obtain a second opinion from an independent surgeon who had no connection with the first doctor.

At first, Alex was irritated by June's suggestion; he wanted to "get it over with so we can go on with our lives."

However, on further reflection, he realized that June had his best interests at heart and he knew that she had more medical knowledge than he possessed. He also felt she was in a better position to evaluate the pros and cons of surgery. So he decided to take her advice and delay his impulsive urge to "get it over with."

With June's help, Alex found an independent surgeon. After the examination and reviewing of x-rays, this doctor told Alex that he disagreed with the other surgeon. He said, "Look, you can always have the surgery. At present there is no emergency; it does not have to be done immediately. Let's see what conservative treatment will do. There are several things that can be tried, such as rest, physical therapy, possibly some medication both oral and by injection and some other measures." June and Alex agreed.

June was pleased that Alex had accepted her advice and had obtained the second opinion. This made June feel that he would respect her opinion in the future, as he had in this instance, and it confirmed her very positive feelings about him.

The ability of each partner to offer and listen to advice is an important basis of every enduring relationship.

25. GENEROUS

This personality trait is crucial, because it goes to the essence of the capacity to be nurturing and caring. In *The Evolution of Desire*, psychologist David Buss explains why ancestral women preferred a generous mate who "may share his meat from the hunt aiding her survival" and helping her children. Modern women are no different and, for good reasons, prefer generous mates, because it benefits the entire nuclear family.[34] A person may be generous in the giving of time, effort and emotional support but very withholding regarding money and other material items. We all know of those who have great wealth but who are skinflints or penny-pinchers. As you think about your relationship, consider these questions: Do you see your prospective spouse as generous or withholding? Will lack of generosity cause conflict? Is the giving of time, effort and emotional support enough despite being tight with money? Is the need to withhold due to early deprivation? Do you see withholding as a control issue? Remember that when events and conditions change (e.g., more income is available), attitudes toward spending may also change.

Usually a person who is generous has the ability to give love and comfort to reduce stress and to be there when needed. Another indication of generosity is the willingness to spend time, money, effort and energy to bring joy and contentment to another human being. It is essential to evaluate this issue of generosity. This positive behavior augurs well when one considers how this person will perform as a spouse, parent and grandparent in the years to come.

Muriel and Ivan were mutually attracted. He was affectionate, intelligent and creative, but he had one trait that really bothered her. Even though he earned an excellent salary, he found it very difficult to spend money. He always chose the least expensive restaurant, he tipped poorly and he even insisted on walking long distances in order to avoid paying for parking. He said, "I just don't like to waste money on valets."

Unfortunately, Muriel didn't have any savings or money of her own. During their marriage she would be dependent on their mutual agreement on most important expenditures. Muriel wondered, *What should I do? I've finally found a guy I care about more than anyone else I dated and I like almost everything about him. But if I marry Ivan, can I accept and live with his penny-pinching behavior?*

Muriel is wise in raising this question before going to the altar with Ivan. If she wants to marry Ivan she must first decide if she can accept Ivan's attitudes concerning the spending of money. After all, financial decisions will have to be made on housing, education of children, vacations and hundreds of other decisions, such as gifts, children's allowances, savings, etc.

Should Muriel go into a marriage knowing that she is bothered by this problem? If she does marry Ivan, she will have been forewarned about possible future conflicts concerning his attitude about money. During the courtship period, Muriel should try to uncover more information about Ivan's early life and what money represented in his formative years. Muriel may become more sympathetic to his scrimping and this could lessen future conflict. Nevertheless, it will be a difficult decision for Muriel.

MUTUAL ELEMENTS OF COMPANIONSHIP

The seven checklist items that we'll focus on next all require mutual agreement or acceptance by both partners. They are unlike the other items, which are personal and unique for each member of the couple. Both the prospective husband and wife should agree and be able to check "YES" on all of the items in this section, whether or not they are red flag items. If any of the seven is a "NO," trouble is possible.

★26. ENJOY TIME TOGETHER

A marital relationship is far more likely to endure if the partners find mutual enjoyment as they spend time alone together. You should be aware of the existence of this type of mutual feeling—or the absence of it—as courtship progresses. We emphasize that this requirement refers to time outside of and away from the bedroom when partners share interests, ideas and discussion of activities and goals. Ask yourself if you look forward to being in close proximity to each other and in providing a "window" into each other's life. This ability to enjoy time with each other is closely related to the essential spouse role of good friend/companion/advisor. If it appears that such feelings of compatibility do not exist when the couple is alone together, a "NO" on this checklist item is most serious. According to Hill, Rubin and Peplau in "Breakups Before Marriage," studies indicate that a primary cause of marital problems is boredom.[35] It is an ominous sign if partners have little to discuss and share with each other and feel that they must look elsewhere for stimulation and companionship. Also note that this is one of our red flag items.

The story of Marna and James reveals a relationship in which compatibility seems a big advantage.

Marna had been going out with James for several months. One night when Marna returned home from her dinner with James, she smiled as she recalled how much she enjoyed their evening together. They had shared gossip about their jobs, heaved mutual sighs about a local scandal and eagerly planned a short vacation together. How easy it was to talk to James. He really listened and responded to her. He was so different from Todd, a previous boyfriend who had been reluctant to discuss or reveal anything personal. Todd always seemed to prefer group settings where sports and other male topics were discussed. And on the occasions when they were alone, at dinner or at other times, Marna recalled there were often long silences and feelings of mutual boredom. But she never felt that way when she was with James.

The marital future of Marna and James is promising. Couples need to understand that the failure to feel mutual joy and satisfaction like Marna and James should cause them to question whether they should continue the relationship. Boredom is the enemy of romance and signals a lack of a most essential ingredient: mutual enjoyment of time spent together, particularly when the couple is alone. Marriages without this key factor rarely endure.

*27. SEXUAL ATTRACTION

Although sex alone is not enough to sustain a marriage, reasonably satisfactory sex, at all ages, is an important part of almost every successful marriage. As the years go by, the intensity and frequency of sexual activity may decrease, although physical closeness and affectionate behavior can continue throughout a couple's lifetime. Social psychologist Ellen Berscheid has written extensively on the relationship between sex, love and marriage and points out in "Whatever Happened to Old Fashioned Lust?" that sexual arousal goes a very long way in romantic love.[36] Sociologists and authors Philip Blumstein and Pepper Schwartz agree and state in *American Couples* that it is their "overwhelming conclusion that a good sex life is central to a good overall relationship."[37]

There is enormous variation with both sexes in the ability to give and receive sexual pleasure. The courtship usually provides ample opportunity for the couple to explore these issues and to decide whether this essential requirement exists. It is also true that sexual satisfaction may be dependent on personal qualities involving kindness, generosity, sensitivity and empathy.

If there are sexual problems during the courtship period, a partner may need to explore, with a professional counselor, past sexual experiences and their effect on the current relationship. Some of these experiences may have been unsatisfying or even traumatic. Dealing with these concerns can improve the couple's sexual pleasure.

Even if a couple decides against sexual consummation before marriage, most will engage in enough intimate physical behavior to determine the presence of or absence of mutual physical attraction.

Often, sexual problems arise during pregnancy. As a wife takes on the additional role of mother, sexual relationships may be altered. Husbands need to be alert to the changes in their wives' sexual behavior in the months before and after the birth of a baby, but these and other sexual difficulties can be overcome with open discussion or professional counseling, if warranted.

Sonya and Harold are a couple who seemed compatible in many areas except that Sonya was not physically attracted to him.

Sonya and Harold met at a church social and found they shared common interests. Sonya didn't know why, but when he tried to kiss her on their fourth date, she instinctively resisted, pushing away. She wasn't sure exactly why she pushed him away and felt guilty in doing so. Sonya liked Harold, but although she could not quite "put her finger on it," she felt no physical attraction to him.

Harold asked her, "What's the matter? Don't you like me?" She completely understood his questioning, because they had been sitting together under a full moon on a beautiful summer evening. It was romantic and conducive to intimacy. Harold's arm had been around her shoulder and they had been enjoying watching the sailboats on the water.

Sonya was silent, reflecting for a while, and then she replied, "Harold, you are a really nice guy and I like you. I'm just not attracted to you in that way. I don't want to hurt your feelings. There's nothing wrong with you. I guess I'm just not the woman for you."

This example illustrates a male/female problem that may occasionally arise: If there is no mutual physical or sexual attraction, most couples will not expect the relationship to proceed toward marriage. If, for instance, a man persists and attempts to show affection but the woman rejects his advances and makes it clear she is not interested or vice versa, that usually signals the end of the relationship.

However, some marriages take place for other reasons even when there is no sexual compatibility. A partner may decide to marry into a wealthy or prominent family. A woman may become pregnant and marry the child's father or an older person may desire an available friend and companion. We believe a truly successful marriage requires mutual "chemistry" and advise you to beware of marrying if your answer to this item is "NO."

*28. AGREEMENT ON MORAL, ETHICAL AND POLITICAL ISSUES

This and the next three "agreement" items could have been titled "No Conflict on Important Issues." Let us first examine item 28, which involves moral, ethical and political beliefs. For example, a male Republican meets a female Democrat and both usually vote their party lines. If both score well on most other items, should a difference in political affiliation be of great concern? The answer depends on whether or not differing political views cause any significant conflict. Even if political views are very different, partners may agree to respect, tolerate, tease and even enjoy each other's point of view.

Other moral and ethical disagreements can be more serious. Let's assume that one partner is concerned about consistent income tax cheating, cheating at cards, minor shoplifting or other illegal or unethical conduct of the other partner. Even though other aspects of their relationship are very positive, this type of basic ethical difference has the serious potential to erode the relationship and cause loss of respect. Rarely, the other partner may decide to accept and live with such questionable behavior. However, concerns about a spouse's honesty and ethics may raise anxiety about sexual fidelity, general management of money, being a model parent and, most of all, trust. Most couples would find it very difficult to reconcile such basic differences concerning morals and ethics. Most marriage authorities, including Wendy Williams and Michael Barnes, who discuss the significance of ethical similarities in "Love Within Life," agree that couples who have similarity of values and beliefs have an increased probability of successful marriage.[38] If there is significant conflict or anxiety over these issues, partners should think carefully before continuing their relationship.

Esther and Eddy are a couple faced with one partner experiencing an ethical dilemma about the other.

Esther and Eddy met at a singles softball game in their local park and dated for several months. One night Eddy invited Esther to accompany him to a local, recently opened restaurant casino. After dinner, Eddy said, "Come with me into the casino and I'll show you how it's possible to have fun and make money at the same time." Esther had never been to a casino before and she was amazed at the vibrant atmosphere, the sounds, the brightly colored lights and the beautiful surroundings. Hundreds of casino patrons were standing or sitting at scores of gaming tables and a variety of electronic gambling machines.

Eddy led her to a blackjack table where she stood behind him as he played. She was amazed how quickly his pile of chips grew and how he seemed to be winning. After about an hour, Eddy said, "Look, it's getting late and you seem tired. Let's go." He walked with Esther over to the cashier and Esther watched as Eddy cashed in over two thousand dollars in chips.

When they were in the car driving back to their homes, Esther said, "You seemed to be a lucky guy tonight; that was a nice stack of chips you cashed in. I don't know much about blackjack, but it looks to me like you know how to play the game. I guess I must have brought you luck."

Eddy smiled and replied, "Well, yes, I do know the game. But I'll confess to you that it wasn't all luck and skill."

"What do you mean?" asked Esther.

"Well," he began, "I have an arrangement with that particular dealer. He sees to it that I win and I split my take with him fifty-fifty."

"But isn't that illegal?" asked Esther.

"Only if you get caught," Eddy replied. "And the best part of it is that I don't even have to pay taxes on the money—there is no record, so I'm in the clear."

Esther was speechless. Up to that point, she had thought that she and Eddy might have a happy future together and she had thought seriously about marrying him. But the blackjack incident convinced her that Eddy did not have the kind of character she was looking for in a spouse. She had been mistaken about him and realized that she and Eddy were finished. Esther always obeyed the law and paid any taxes that she owed. She knew she could never respect or live with any man lacking in such basic moral values.

Esther asked herself, *What kind of moral example would he set for our children? Would he teach them to cheat at cards? For all I know, he might be unfaithful to me, although I haven't had that feeling up to this point. This trip to the casino was certainly an eye-opener.*

This example underscores the need for couples to spend at least six months or more together and to be involved in many different activities prior to marriage. Eddy's illegal behavior may not have come to light if theirs had been a "whirlwind romance" followed by early marriage.

*29. AGREEMENT ON MAJOR GOALS: HAVING A FAMILY, RELIGIOUS AFFILIATION, CHILDCARE

These areas and how each partner feels concerning these long-range goals are most crucial to explore during a courtship and before marriage. Agreement will help to strengthen the relationship and diminish potential stress. For example, if both the future husband and wife agree that they don't want to have children or they both agree that they want to have a family and look forward to the parenting process, it is a definite plus for their future relationship. However, if the wife wishes to have children and the husband does not (or vice versa), this has the potential to create major disappointment and argument. Other issues include the number of children to have and educational goals for the children. Should they attend public, private or parochial schools?

Religion is another area where conflict may arise, especially if one person wishes to imbue in their children a strong belief in a particular faith, but the other partner strongly disapproves of this religion or is an agnostic or atheist and rejects children having religious education, training or affiliation.

Who should work and who should care for the children is another subject that must be discussed. A woman may wish to stay home and care for her children, but her husband may want her to work to supplement the family income or so he can stay home and act as the primary caregiver for the children, a trend that has increased to more than two million stay-at-home fathers in the United States.[39] Both partners may want to work and disagree on outside childcare: grandparents, a nanny, day care or something else.

Sociologists and authors Blumstein and Schwartz discuss in some detail partners' agreement or disagreement on goals, including raising a family and whether both parents should work, and their effect on children. They also explore the need for parental care of children, as opposed to substitute care.[40] For many couples, such issues can be explosive. If there is disagreement in any of these areas, it is important to explore the intensity of the feelings and the rigidity with which partners hold these beliefs or opinions. Again, flexibility comes into the picture. Couples who cannot resolve these issues in premarital discussions should be wary of marrying.

It is helpful to observe how differing opinions are handled. Does each partner listen? Can each consider the other's point of view? Or does one or both leave the discussion feeling diminished or degraded?

If conflict is very intense and certain goals are held rigidly, there may be serious problems in the marriage, but if the opposing view is not strongly held it may be possible, after discussion, to reconcile, compromise or eliminate the conflict. However, it is very dangerous to postpone exploring any of these issues. They need to be faced and this should be done early in the relationship so partners can enter marriage with the issues resolved. Discussion will help a couple to decide if their relationship should continue or end.

Clarice and Cyrus are a couple who avoided facing their mixed feelings about becoming parents in their early relationship.

Clarice and Cyrus planned to get married. Their sexual relations were great, they enjoyed each other's company and they had talked a lot about their future plans, but, unfortunately, there was one real area of disagreement from Clarice's viewpoint. She wanted to have children, but Cyrus made it very clear to her that he did not, under any circumstances, want to be a father. He told her, "I'm not interested in raising children. I know how you feel about it and I wish I could see it your way, but I don't and I don't want you to misunderstand me on this issue."

However, Clarice and Cyrus were very attracted to each other and were compatible in every other part of their lives. They decided not to discuss this one item. Clarice thought to herself, *Well, I really love this guy and I don't know when I'm going to find anybody else like him. So I think I'm going to take a chance. I will get married and maybe he and I will figure this thing out later.*

They married and for the first few months everything went well. Both had good jobs; they set up housekeeping and did not talk about the "problem." Sex still was wonderful and the weeks went by.

Then Clarice began to worry. She said to herself, *I can't go on like this.* She resolved to raise the issue of having children with Cyrus. One day she told him, "Cyrus, we're getting along fine. I'm very happy with our marriage, but I'm becoming obsessed with wanting a baby and I can't stop thinking about it. What can I do? I want to have a baby and I know you don't agree, so let's take another look at this. Can't we agree to have at least one child and see how it goes?"

Cyrus looked grim and did not reply for a long moment. Then he said, "Look, Clarice, I told you at the beginning of our relationship that I never want to bring a child into this world. Now I can see that we just are not going to be able to agree about this." Then he walked out of the room and shut the door behind him.

Cyrus and Clarice are heading into trouble. It will be difficult to resolve this conflict and it appears that the marriage will have serious problems. It would have been beneficial had Cyrus and Clarice explored this problem in greater depth during their courtship period. She may have discovered the reasons why Cyrus was so adamant about not wanting children. Perhaps he was concerned about passing health problems on to the next generation or associated childbirth with a traumatic event. His mother may have died in childbirth giving birth to a sibling. He may have been the oldest of seven children and already parented a brood of infants. Perhaps Clarice would have accepted his decision if she had explored his reasoning and history.

The conflict between Cyrus and Clarice illustrates the absolute necessity of husband and wife agreeing on major issues, such as children, religion and parenting. Some wives in Clarice's position go to the extreme and contrive a way to have a child, gambling on the fact that their husbands may "come around" to the idea and accept the child. However, this can cause further disagreement and pain. We suggest that before a couple marries they agree on major goals.

30. AGREEMENT ON MONEY MANAGEMENT AND INVESTMENTS

One of the four important roles that are involved in every marriage is that of business partner. Checklist item 8: Adequate or Potential Assets/Income deals with the requirement of a prospective mate to provide for the family. But equally as important as adequacy of income and assets is the need for the partners to agree about their management. How much to save? How much to spend? And on what should the money be spent?

During the dating and engagement period, couples should focus on questions such as: Is he or she only happy when dining at expensive restaurants or buying expensive clothes? Does he or she seem to have a weakness for the latest computer gadget? Does he or she display good judgment about conserving income? Do we agree on the scale and cost of our wedding? Should we buy a luxury car, an inexpensive model or a motorcycle? Most important: Are we able to discuss the pros and cons of purchases and investments? Financial matters should be carefully discussed and agreed upon well before a decision to marry. Beware of marriage when you have fundamental differences with your partner about how you will handle money when married. By the time a couple is ready to walk down the aisle, they should either be in agreement on financial goals or be aware of and accept the differences. Sociologists and authors Blumstein and Schwartz discuss in their book *American Couples* how money management can be "a source of conflict" between husband and wife.

They point out that once the couple marries, both lose "complete financial independence." Joint decision making is required and other qualities such as flexibility come into play.[41] Income, investments and spending needs may vary greatly over the years. The ability to discuss and face these issues openly is vital to future harmony in the relationship.

Connie and Jesse are partners who illustrate the benefits of paying attention to differing financial points of view.

Connie grew up in poverty. At times, her family was barely able to feed Connie and her two sisters. But Connie was unusually intelligent, ambitious and determined to avoid the stresses of her early childhood. She excelled at school and earned a full scholarship to an Ivy League college. After college, she was extremely successful as an executive in a real estate company. She met Jesse, a young research physician, when he was in the process of buying a condominium. Their relationship began with lunches, then dinners and finally serious dating. He earned a reasonable salary but was uninterested in financial matters; he was focused on his work in medical research.

During their courtship, Connie discussed the pros and cons of various investments and real estate opportunities and while Jesse listened politely, it was clear that he could not work up any real interest in these topics. Otherwise, the couple was very compatible and shared many other common interests. They enjoyed attending lectures and discussion groups. They were very happy to spend time together and were never bored. The romance flourished.

About a week prior to their wedding, during one evening when they were having dinner, Jesse said, frowning, "Connie, I've had something on my mind for quite awhile and I think this is a good time before our wedding to get it off my chest."

Connie was concerned. "Sweetheart, is something wrong? You seem so serious."

Jesse smiled and said, "I just wanted to ask you something and I didn't know how you'd react, that's all."

"You know you can talk to me about anything," Connie replied.

"Okay," he said. "After we're married, I wondered if it would be okay if you would take charge of our finances: our checking account, investments and savings. These are items that I am uncomfortable dealing with. I've noticed you seem very interested in our financial affairs and handling money issues. I'm not into that aspect of our life. That's what I wanted to talk to you about. What do you say?"

Connie was relieved. "Of course I will. You can focus on your medical research projects. I can see how important they are to you. I promise that I'll discuss all major financial decisions with you before taking action. For example, I would like to save money for a house with a large backyard before we have children, but for now the condo is great."

Jesse, who had grown up in the country, was thrilled with Connie's plan. He leaned across the table to clasp and squeeze her hand.

This is a realistic example of a couple who made a premarital decision concerning who would handle their finances. It is not essential that there be such an explicit definition of financial roles like the discussion between Jesse and Connie, but it is essential that partners entering marriage gain some insight into each spouse's approach to money matters and then mutually agree on their respective roles in the smooth handling of income and outgo. They should also discuss possible long-range expenditures. Should they save money to buy an apartment or house? Should their future children go to public or private school? How much money should be put away for a "rainy day"? There should be basic mutual agreement on money matters before a couple weds.

31. AGREEMENT CONCERNING PETS

It may seem strange to some to think that pets have anything to do with spouse selection. But pet issues have been known to strain or even destroy relationships. For example, the male owner of a beloved dog should not assume that his future wife will welcome the animal into the home the new couple will create, because she may actually hate or fear dogs. The same problem might exist if a woman is very attached to her pet cats; perhaps her new spouse is allergic to cats and becomes ill with contact. It may be that a couple does not have a pet at the time of courtship but may want to adopt one when married or when the children are old enough to enjoy them. The subject of pets needs to be explored and discussed and a harmonious and mutual agreement should be reached during the dating/courting process. If the pet issue escalates and is not easily resolved, it may be indicative of other major marital problem areas. It may be easier for partners to fight over a pet issue than explore tensions over household disorder or other conflicts.

Jason and Erika had differing ideas on the importance of pets that affected their relationship.

Jason was often jealous of the affection that Erika lavished upon her dog Sandy. She seemed to express great empathy and concern for Sandy, who was a beautiful golden retriever. Jason wished that he could enjoy the same physical contact and warmth from Erika as she snuggled and hugged Sandy. Jason also admired the nurturing qualities that Erika displayed toward her dog and he felt that she would probably prove to be a very loving wife and parent.

However, one day he did share with Erika his feelings of envy about Sandy and said, "I wish I could get more of those spontaneous hugs and kisses that you shower on Sandy."

Erika was surprised and jumped up to embrace him, planting an enthusiastic kiss on his lips. "Thank you for letting me in on your honest feelings. Jason, you will always come first."

Attachment to a pet can be profound. As with Erika and Jason, potential conflict over pets can usually be resolved quickly.

32. ACCEPTANCE OF MATCH BY BOTH FAMILIES

If both families are delighted with the prospective union, this can provide support for the relationship and validate the wisdom of the decision to marry. These new extended families can act as a positive force, extending warmth and affection to the couple. On the other hand, such enthusiastic acceptance has its negatives: A spouse seeker may not trust his or her own perceptions and be impelled into an unwise marriage because of the family's strong endorsement of the union.

The possible consequences of a family's endorsement of a couple can be seen in the relationship of William and Marilyn.

William's mother and father "just loved" Marilyn and her family. They encouraged William to propose, telling him not only was she smart and attractive, but also her father was very prominent and would help William in his career.

Despite this pressure, William began to have serious doubts about the relationship. He became aware of Marilyn's irritability. Then, as they spent more time together, he noticed she had episodes of food bingeing and depression. He began to feel more and more agitated about spending an evening with Marilyn and dreaded having to constantly cheer her up and reassure her that he loved her. He had his doubts and was glad he hadn't yet asked her to marry him. But he also feared having to tell his parents there would be no marriage. They were so looking forward to the union of the two families and to future grandchildren.

Fortunately, William had the strength and good judgment to reject the advice of his parents and to end the relationship.

The story of William and Marilyn illustrates that families can play an important positive or negative role in influencing the marital choices of their sons and daughters. William wisely decided not to follow the wishes of his mother and father. In time his parents would most likely accept his decision, once they understood the reason for the breakup.

No matter how well matched partners may be, they should never underestimate the importance of the opinions of their respective families concerning their relationship. Much of the literature discussing family attitudes concerning children's marriages focuses on interracial, interreligious and intercultural marriages. Even in this third millennium, many families retain "deeply ingrained attitudes that have become part of their psyche," according to the article "How to Deal with Your Family if They Do Not Accept Your Date."[42] Strong family disapproval can be a corrosive influence and can inflict enormous conflict and stress on the relationship that may result in the loss of both emotional and financial support of the families involved. Families' attitudes may influence a difficult choice or decision to be made: Do I listen to my own judgment or that of my family?

Ultimately, although a parent's opinion should certainly be considered, it should not be any more controlling than other positive or negative factors. Each family and couple is unique. Whether or not a family's attitudes and opinions will—or should—affect the future marriage will differ in every situation. We advise couples to realistically acknowledge such family attitudes (if they exist) and decide if the relationship can survive rejection by one or both families. The decision may not be easy.

OTHER PROBLEM AREAS

Two of the last three items are red flags that can carry serious implications. While major physical problems may be obvious, emotional and psychological illnesses may not be easily discerned. Addictions as well as past or present criminal or civil litigation may also be hard to determine early in the courtship. Therefore a long courtship with ample time for discovery will provide the best opportunity to explore these issues.

*33. NO ADDICTION TO SMOKING, ALCOHOL, DRUGS OR GAMBLING

Addiction is habitual activity that is difficult to change and also has negative effects not only on the addicted person, but also on those close to him or her. While occasional cigarette smoking, alcohol consumption and even recreational drug use may be tolerable, habitual and compulsive use of these substances is often stressful or even fatal to a relationship and future family. Addictive behavior tends to exclude the needs of others and focuses on the satisfaction of the person involved. The previous example of Joan and Gary demonstrates how problematic alcohol and gambling behavior can impact a relationship and how important it is to resolve such issues prior to marriage.

Unfortunately, addictive behavior may not be apparent early in the dating and courtship period and strong attachments may already have been formed by the time it is discovered. One coping mechanism may be to postpone formal engagement and marriage until the partner demonstrates a resolve to face and handle his or her addictions.

Some persons have lived with parents with addictions and feel they can deal with these issues. They claim they are comfortable with this kind of negative behavior. But for most spouse seekers, intractable drug, alcohol or gambling addictions may be the most dangerous of our red flag factors. Despite the fact that facing these problems may be emotionally wrenching, it is usually best if the non-addicted partner terminates the relationship sooner, not later, in the dating and courtship period.

Smoking

Heavy smokers are candidates for many personal health problems and such an addiction also poses serious risks to those close to the smoker. Many will tolerate this habit and accept such risks, since the effects of smoking may not become evident in the early years of marriage. But it is important that the smoker be aware of the impact on him or herself as well as on his or her family and attempt to modify this behavior. Even President Obama has attempted to quit smoking at the request of his wife. For some, it is understandable that the relationship could end unless there is a serious effort to control or modify this addiction.

Early in the dating process one partner may light up a cigarette. He or she may or may not ask permission if he or she can smoke. The other partner needs to question: How many cigarettes a day do you smoke? When did you start smoking? Do you plan to quit? Have you tried to stop in the past? Are you aware of the many health problems associated with smoking? Did your parents smoke?

Two smokers, Evan and Ellen, were in a romantic relationship.

Evan and Ellen both began smoking in their teens and had met in a smoking area outside of the office building where they were employed. Their romance blossomed and during courting their mutual smoking addiction did not appear to be an issue. However, as their romance became more intense and they discussed marriage and family plans, Ellen felt they could no longer ignore their smoking problem.

"Evan," she said while they were having dinner together, "you know I'm in the insurance business. I have been reviewing the alarming impact of smoking on longevity, health and children who are exposed to secondary smoke by their parents. Since we agree we are going to have children, I don't see how we dare continue our smoking habit. We need to decide how we can deal with it. Remember, it isn't only our children, but it's our own health prospects. After all, children need healthy parents, not ones who are candidates for lung cancer, emphysema or chronic obstructive pulmonary disease. How do you feel about this?"

Evan was quick to reply. "I've been concerned myself and I realize I've just been avoiding the problem. In fact, now I am up to about a pack a day and I know it should stop. I think both of us must figure out how to quit and we should do it together."

Ellen agreed and offered to do research on how they could best approach the problem and give up smoking. "I know it won't be easy—I've tried before—but together maybe we can do it." Evan agreed.

Fortunately, both Evan and Ellen agreed on a plan to end this dangerous habit and potential source of conflict. The odds of success are far better in such a situation as opposed to one where the prospective husband and wife do not agree about how to fight their addictions. Providing mutual support is helpful.

Couples may find they are very compatible on most of the important marital issues and they may elect to overlook or "live with" a smoking problem. This may be true whether it involves one or both partners. But such couples need to attempt to look years ahead. All may go well until children arrive. Partners should realize that when children arrive, they will require parents who are healthy, willing and able to nurture them through their growing years. They should consider the problems and effects of secondhand smoke on their children. Partners might discuss: Will smoking become an issue when children arrive? Before entering marriage the couple should also consider whether or not this issue will cause stress and be a source of future marital conflict, even though smoking's long-range consequences may not arise for a number of years. Parental smoking, like other events from early childhood, may have delayed effects.

Alcohol and Drugs
Addictions to these substances are a major cause of marital strife and divorce. Persons under the influence of alcohol can be physically and verbally abusive and often have difficulty in sustaining employment. They are more susceptible to accidents and illness. It is also a difficult addiction to modify and there is a high rate of recidivism.[43] The same is true regarding prescription as well as illegal drug use. Habitual use

of heroin, cocaine, amphetamines and other drugs can be dangerous and inflict serious physical and psychological damage. Depending on the extent of their drug use, at times parents can be incapable of protecting and nurturing their children. They also can become abusive or neglectful when under the influence of drugs or alcohol. There is a significant intergenerational effect of alcoholism in families and it is important to explore with a partner whether or not his or her parents were addicted to alcohol or other substances. Unfortunately, exploring these issues can be difficult. Most people deny their addictions and are often offended by even the suggestion that they have a problem. Signs of excessive drinking or drug use mandate extreme caution in continuing with a relationship.

Denial of an addiction became apparent and troublesome to Danny in his relationship with Selma.

Selma taught preschool and returned to her apartment at about four o'clock most afternoons, exhausted from the active four-year-olds in her class. Often she needed a drink and on one particular day when she had plans to go out later, she immediately poured herself a glass of wine and then another, collapsing on the sofa in front of the television set. Later that evening after a few more glasses of wine, she met her new boyfriend Danny, who was a marriage counselor at a neighborhood clinic. When they got to their favorite pizzeria, they both ordered a beer and before the salad arrived, Selma ordered a second. Selma's speech was becoming slurred. This night they planned to join friends at a bar and listen to a visiting band. Danny was a little concerned, because on their last date he noticed that Selma drank several martinis. He was worried about her driving home.

Although Danny was reluctant to bring up the issue of Selma's drinking with her, his concerns were growing. So he began to question her about her own family and what they liked to drink. He asked her whether their use of alcohol affected her siblings. She mentioned how late at night as a teenager she shared a glass of wine with her dad. It was a very special alone time. However, she admitted that drinking caused her father to lose his business and that he eventually abandoned her mother.

Danny was glad they began the discussion, because he was increasingly concerned that Selma needed to gain some insight and help with what seemed to be a problem with alcohol. That night he drove her home, as she seemed too tipsy to drive safely by herself. As much as he was attracted to Selma, he was aware of the problems she faced in dealing with her seeming addiction. A large part of his practice was treating clients with addictive issues. He was not sure he would continue the relationship, because he knew how difficult it would be for Selma to face and overcome this problem. He recognized the issue as a red flag and was unsure how to face it.

Gambling

An addicted gambler can deprive his family of regular income and can easily dissipate family assets no matter how substantial. However, if a spouse prospect is otherwise desirable and if he or she is motivated and gets help, the gambling addiction may be controlled. Nevertheless, as with the other addictions discussed, such spouse prospects should be viewed as very questionable life partners.

*34. NO MAJOR PHYSICAL, MENTAL OR EMOTIONAL HEALTH PROBLEMS

Illness, whether physical or emotional, adds stress to any relationship. Whether a prospective partner is young or older, health issues require exploration. Some of these problems are perceived early, such as orthopedic disabilities and obesity, but others, such as diabetes, heart trouble, genetic diseases or even infertility, may not be apparent until after marriage. Nonetheless, there are definite clues that give an indication of health problems and it is important to remain alert during the courtship and dating period. Watch and observe what medicines a potential spouse takes. If he or she mentions repeated doctor visits and hospitalizations in the past, ask: "Why were you sick or hospitalized?" Be observant when you eat together and inquire if you notice any unusual dietary habits. Also, you should notice if the prospective spouse has a general sense of vigor and vitality or if he or she appears constantly tired or depressed.

Health issues may become even more important with older prospective mates, because age usually increases physical ailments and disabilities. But the key inquiry should always be: how will his or her health issues affect our relationship? Then you must consider if you, as a spouse seeker, are willing to accept the prospective spouse despite the health problems.

If the future mate has the potential to be seriously ill, a spouse seeker should honestly deliberate his or her ability to act as a caregiver. Will taking on the role of caretaker create a feeling of panic or revulsion? Some partners may actually enjoy giving support to and nurturing their mates.

Fran and Ted are a couple who faced serious health issues.

Fran was a registered nurse working in the renal unit of a large hospital. Ted, who was a lawyer, was in the hospital for removal of a diseased kidney. His surgery had gone well and the two met during the postsurgical period when Fran helped care for Ted. After Ted's discharge from the hospital, Fran made home visits to him under a program that her hospital had instituted. A romance blossomed and Fran began to think, *Is Ted a realistic marital prospect for me? Will the removal of his kidney influence his longevity? Will he wind up in dialysis or will his health issues be resolved?*

Later that year Ted proposed marriage and Fran realized that she had to make a decision. She really liked Ted and knew he would be an excellent husband and father. But she wondered about his odds of living a normal life and becoming a father, among other questions.

Fran's problem is not simple. She is realistic and aware of the issues. As a nurse, she is probably in a better position to answer these questions as compared to the average person. However, illness or disability not only can put stress on a marriage but also may result in the premature death of a parent. Illness and death often can jeopardize the other spouse's quality of life and that of the entire family if the couple has children. The family may be deprived of parental and spousal support if one marital partner should become seriously ill or deceased.

We suggest that if a prospective partner has a major illness or disability, a spouse seeker should carefully consider such issues before making a final marital decision. The best time to discuss these medical issues and questions is over the weeks and months of dating and courtship.

35. NO MAJOR PAST OR PRESENT LEGAL PROBLEMS

If a prospective spouse has served considerable jail time or is involved in many lawsuits, further inquiry is essential. Is he or she hostile, combative or immoral? Was the future mate embroiled in many criminal or ethical conflicts? The time to explore these issues is well before marriage. Throughout the United States, many courts have easily accessible records of both civil and criminal activity. Today, most of these records can easily be found online and printed from a computer. If you possess reasonable computer skills, it should not be necessary to employ expert help to discover the legal past of a prospective mate. If you are uncomfortable about your computer ability, find a friend or relative to help you. If you'd prefer to keep the matter confidential, many firms have computer experts for hire. The one area where you may need help is inquiry about a criminal record including convictions, jail time, etc. If you are concerned about negative issues, particularly crimes involving a prospective mate, get in touch with the local police or sheriff and, if your locality permits it, you can inquire about records of criminal activity.

Insofar as non-criminal legal matters are involved, such as lawsuits about money, fraud, civil assault, battery, negligence or drunk driving, you may wish to consult an attorney to help with your inquiry. All of these inquiries can be done on a confidential basis.

Be aware that in today's litigious society there are many lawsuits that are valid and others which are bogus. The mere fact that a prospective spouse has sued or been sued will rarely disqualify him or her as a potential mate. But a repetitive record of lawsuits should raise questions in your mind. Your best bet for finding out about these problems is a long courtship and engagement period.

One couple we focused on, Doug and Suzette, exhibit how such issues need to be addressed prior to marriage.

Doug and Suzette had started to date after meeting at a Little League game. Both were divorced and each had a son in the game. Suzette found Doug friendly and compatible. After a few months of dating, it became clear that the relationship was becoming much more than casual.

At dinner one evening, Doug told her, "Look, Suzette, I want to tell you some things about my history. I served six months in county jail for assault and battery. This was five years ago and the incident was the cause of my divorce. I hit my wife in a fit of uncontrolled anger. I know I was at fault and I realized that, so since my release five years ago, I have continued my participation in an anger management class. I believe this kind of anger is behind me, but I felt you should know about it."

Suzette was shocked but was grateful for Doug's candor and honesty. Although they'd only been dating three months, she had noticed that he could be difficult and oppositional at times and could easily provoke a confrontation. But she also realized that she should take lots of time to observe Doug and test their relationship. She knew that she had to think about her son as well as herself. But she felt hopeful; she had very positive feelings about Doug, who was open and honest in revealing his anger issues and criminal record.

In fact, Suzette is wise in proceeding carefully with Doug and in taking ample time to determine if he has overcome his anger problem. This is precisely what a long period of courtship and engagement will provide. This example also demonstrates why a previous criminal conviction should not automatically disqualify an otherwise acceptable spouse prospect. It may be that Doug can or already has overcome this unfortunate tendency to violence from his past and that his stint in jail was a positive experience. But only time will tell if his episodes of uncontrolled anger are behind him. The decision as to whether to keep dating Doug may not be an easy one for Suzette, who is also concerned about Doug acting as stepfather to her son.

SELF-EVALUATION

The checklist not only gives you a format for evaluating a possible mate, but it also serves as a self-evaluation. Now that you understand the checklist, it becomes appropriate for you to apply it to yourself (except for items 26 through 32 which must await the selection of a possible mate). Consider your answers and note which items you score as "NO." Completion of these items will help sharpen your awareness, both of the evaluation process and of your own possible problem areas.

chapter four

Applying the Checklist to a Relationship

We will explore how Joan, whose relationship with Gary we discussed in an earlier chapter, could have used the checklist to evaluate Gary. We will assume that Joan herself is relatively free of red flag items, such as addictions, inability to control anger, major health problems, poor attachment experiences, etc. However, if she finds that she does not fulfill one or more of the important requirements to create a stable and fulfilling marriage, it behooves her to work on these negative issues. She may need to gain insight and face those personality traits that could sabotage a committed relationship. If these problems do exist, individual or group therapy may help Joan modify her behavior and better prepare her to function as a successful mate.

RECONFIGURING THE STORY OF JOAN AND GARY

Now we will retell the story of Gary and Joan and learn how Joan should have handled her relationship with Gary. This time, during her early relationship with Gary, Joan has a copy of the Prospective Spouse Checklist. Joan has decided she is going to use her head as well as her heart in evaluating Gary and herself as possible spouses. Don't forget that Joan's completion of Gary's checklist is only part of the spouse selection process. As we have indicated, she must also complete the same checklist process for herself, because spouse selection is a mutual, two-way task.

As you read this revised version, contrast it with how Joan, in our earlier telling of the story (chapter 2), was basically unaware of many factors and unprepared for her marriage to Gary.

Joan was outgoing and social, with many female friends. Some were happily married; others, after short marriages, were already divorced. Still others were seeing marriage counselors and had confided to Joan that their marriages were going badly. Joan, like most single young men and women, was hoping her current dating partner was the "right" mate and they would marry "once and for keeps."

After enjoying several dates with Gary, Joan decided it was time to examine and fill out the Prospective Spouse Checklist. *Some of these items I have already considered. But I'm not sure why some of the others are even included. Like why should family history be important, since it mostly involves the very early years of life? I guess I'd better find out why the checklist includes some of these items so that I can understand what the "YES" or "NO" answers mean for my choice of a husband.*

First Joan reviewed the descriptions of each checklist item and answered them for herself. After Joan filled out her copy of the checklist she thought, *I'm glad I now have some insight and guidelines about how best to evaluate my new relationship and why each of these items is included in the checklist. Now I'm going to start again at the first item and see how much I know about Gary.*

Items 1 through 8 were easy for Joan and she put a check mark in each "YES" box. Gary was single, had no children and had no previous marriages. Their ages were quite close—only two years difference—and so were their educations and intelligence levels. They were the same race and religion; both were Methodists. She was also confident that both would be able to earn adequate incomes, as Gary had already lined up a job with a well-known company.

But when she arrived at the Family History section her brow furrowed. She realized that on their first dates she and Gary did not even think about discussing what happened when they were infants and toddlers or any of the other subjects covered by these items. As she scanned the other items remaining, she said: "I'd better make sure we explore these areas of his life on future dates." She was confident that their relationship would continue: she could tell that Gary was interested in her and would be "in touch" as he said he would. She thought, *I'll have plenty of time to go over the rest of the checklist after I know him a little bit better.* She sighed happily.

Gary called soon after and asked her to have dinner with him the next night at a neighborhood dining and dancing spot. She agreed enthusiastically and could hardly wait.

As she sat down at the table in the restaurant the next night, she said to herself, *Take it easy. Don't scare this guy off. Be cool.*

They ordered dinner and then Gary said to Joan, "What are you so pensive about?"

Joan paused and then responded, "Well, after our last date, I realized I would like to know more: where you live, about your family, what is fun for you, what has been difficult in your life and what you were like growing up. How about telling me a little bit about your early life and I'll do the same, if you're interested."

Gary replied, "You bet I'm interested and since you asked, I'll go first."

Gary told her that his mom and dad were divorced when he was about three or four and that for a time his father lived nearby and he saw him frequently. He was forced to stay overnight with his father on weekends even though he was afraid, because his father yelled a lot and usually had a strange woman living with him. Gary remembered that he cried a lot and after a while his father told him he could not stand a crybaby. Gary's mom tried to comfort him when he told her that he didn't like to stay overnight with his dad, but she explained that the judge said he had to go even if he didn't want to. Then his dad moved away to a distant city and Gary did not see him again. He recalled that his mom had to work full-time to support him and his older sister. As they continued to discuss his childhood, Gary told Joan that he recalled that his mom was always kind to him, but when she got home from work, she always seemed to be carrying around a drink and sometimes acted weird and then usually slept for what seemed like a long time.

After hearing this, Joan was silent for a few moments and then thought to herself, *This is really good. I know a lot more about Gary to help me with the checklist, but I don't think I will mention anything about the list to Gary—at least not now.*

By this time they had finished dinner and ordered dessert. Dance music began to waft out of the speakers. It was one of those old-fashioned ballroom numbers from the forties or fifties—a long time before either of them was born. Gary said, "Would you like to dance while we're waiting for dessert?"

"Sure," replied Joan. Gary took her hand, leading her to the dance floor.

"This is why I picked this place," said Gary. "I hope you like dancing."

"Well, I'll give it a try," replied Joan. Smiling, Gary put his arm around her waist and pulled her close. It felt both comfortable and exciting as their bodies met. Gary was an excellent dancer and led very well. She could tell as he held her gently but quite firmly. She relaxed as they glided across the dance floor. *Gary is terrific,* she thought. *I like him.* They talked about all sorts of things and Joan was particularly intrigued when Gary told her that someday he hoped to find a wife and have a family.

Later that evening, Gary bid her goodbye at the door to her apartment, saying, "I'll call you tomorrow." And Joan could sense that he really meant it.

As soon as the door closed, she made a beeline for her Prospective Spouse Checklist. She noticed that so far she had completed only items 1 through 8. *Now*, she thought, *I have quite a bit of family history information for items 9 through 14. Let's see how much I can complete.* She looked at item 9: Well Treated, Loved and Nurtured in Early Years and realized that she really didn't have enough knowledge—even now—to check "YES" or "NO" so she decided to leave it blank and obtain more information in the future. Although she did know that his mom worked, she had no idea how many caregivers Gary had up to age three. So, she also left item 10: Same Caregiver(s) to Age Three blank, but on item 11: Parents Remained Married Through Teen Years, she checked "NO" since she had found out that his parents had divorced when Gary was about four years old.

Joan was uncertain about item 12: Good Relationships with Parents, Siblings and Grandparents. She knew that Gary had told her that he had a close, positive relationship with Sue, his older sister. It also seemed that he and his mom got along very well, except for her "weird" times when she was drinking and doing a lot of sleeping. However, it was clear to Joan that if his relationship with his father was the only consideration, it should be a definite "NO." Nonetheless, Joan figured, "It's two against one, so I'll check 'YES'." This illustrates the difficulty when making "YES" or "NO" decisions about personal questions: often it is hard to be sure what answer to give. It also illustrates why spouse selection cannot ultimately be decided by tallying up and comparing the number of "YES" and "NO" items.

In view of the divorce of Gary's parents when he was so

young, Joan checked "NO" on item 13: Observed Affection Between Parents. She also checked "NO" on item 14: Parents: Good Physical/Emotional Health, No Major Alcohol, Drug or Other Problems, because Gary had described his mother's drinking problem.

Joan lay on her bed for a long while after finishing what she could on the Family History section. *There's a lot I still need to know about this guy,* she thought. But she was confident she could obtain the information. Then she started to think about the next section: Personality Traits/Behavior. She realized that after several dates, she already had answers to more of the items. Without hesitation, she checked "YES" on items 15: Kind and Considerate, 16: Sense of Humor, 17: Cheerful and 18: Has Friends, because she felt that her discussions with Gary had given her enough knowledge to do so. And she realized that, if it turned out that she had made a mistake, she could always change her answers.

She paused when she arrived at item 19: Mature Judgment. She realized that she had no idea how she should answer this question. After all, they had only been together on a few dates. Also, she had not even thought of gathering this kind of information during the previous times she had been together with Gary. The same was true concerning most of the remaining items. She checked "YES" on item 26: Enjoy Time Together. Joan was confident about the answer, because there had been lots of fun with Gary. She also admitted to herself that it definitely felt like she would very shortly be checking "YES" on item 27: Sexual Attraction.

Joan was thrilled with the momentum of her new romance. There were several more dates that were a lot of fun: movies, dinners alone together and with friends and, best of all, they had begun to study together. They were both in their last semester before getting their MBAs and both had to be ready for their upcoming final exams. Joan felt like she was really learning much more about Gary as they spoke and took occasional breaks from their studies. She also realized that she really enjoyed being with him no matter what they were doing. She tried to put her finger on the reason for this. It took her a while, because it was a gut feeling that was not easy to verbalize, but she knew it was a lot more than physical chemistry. She finally concluded that Gary made her feel satisfied, as if she had successfully completed an important project. It was similar to the feeling she had had when she won a prestigious academic competition and was awarded a prize in high school. Then, finally, she realized she felt she really had—in a sense—won a prize: a man who just might be the kind of person for whom she had been searching a long time. She decided to watch Gary, encourage him and work on their relationship.

Whenever she had the chance she took out Gary's checklist and looked to see if she could check more boxes. Within a few more weeks she felt it was time to check "YES" on item 19: Mature Judgment. Gary definitely seemed much more mature than many of the guys she had dated. He had realistic plans for the future: to work in computer software sales where he said he saw much opportunity. He told Joan, "I may not be Bill Gates, but there are thousands of new software programs being developed all over the world. I plan to be involved in the sales and distribution of these applications." And Gary already had a job lined up with a midsized corporation where he was to start work shortly after he received his MBA.

One day after class, Gary said, "Say, I've got a great idea. Why don't you come over to my apartment tonight after we have dinner? We can study together there instead of at the library."

Joan's heart skipped a beat. This was exciting, because it meant more concentrated time alone with Gary. "Okay," she said. "It's a deal! And guess what? I'll cook dinner for you too."

"Great," Gary replied.

After class, Joan quickly shopped for ingredients, arrived at Gary's apartment and immediately went to work in the kitchen while Gary started studying in the living room. After about ten minutes, Joan heard Gary come into the kitchen. He was smiling.

"What's so funny?" she asked.

Gary answered, "You're pretty as a picture—just like those girls in those t-shirt ads." Joan looked down and noticed that her thin cotton t-shirt was wet from her food preparation and clung to her breasts. She blushed and before she knew it, Gary had taken her in his arms and pressed his mouth against hers. Joan's lips parted and her arms went around his neck. She felt their bodies come together and knew Gary was very aroused. Hand in hand, they moved to the bedroom, dinner temporarily forgotten. Their clothes were tossed on the bedroom floor as they hungrily found pleasure in each other. She felt intense enjoyment as their lovemaking continued. Gary was considerate and passionate, yet gentle.

Exhausted, they pressed together. Gary whispered in Joan's ear, "I hoped we could go on like that for hours." Joan, still basking in the afterglow, nodded in silent agreement and squeezed even closer to Gary.

She thought to herself, *Now I get to check "YES" on the item for sexual attraction.*

As they climbed out of bed and dressed, Gary said, "You know, we've got three days off this holiday weekend. Let's go to Las Vegas and pick up where we're leaving off today."

"Good idea," Joan replied. As soon as she arrived back at her apartment, she firmly checked the "YES" box on item 27.

The next day, Joan had trouble concentrating. She kept thinking about the delicious evening she had spent with Gary and their upcoming three days in Las Vegas, where she knew there would be lots of time for encores of the previous night.

In thinking about how things had been going with Gary during the past weeks and months, she found that she and Gary had many areas of common interest, such as current political events. She had always felt that she kept herself well informed and was very impressed that Gary seemed to know much more than she did about all sorts of governmental problems. She also appreciated the fact that Gary seemed willing to explain his positions and did not hesitate to change an opinion if he learned new facts.

She also found out more about Gary's early life: how his mother had managed to stay home and care for him until he was a year old and that she had to borrow money to do this. Then Joan discovered that Gary's grandmother had taken care of him until he was almost ready for kindergarten. Gary also told her that when he found a wife, he hoped that she would stay home and take care of their children when they were young and not put them in day care. This coincided with Joan's own ideas on the subject and she said to herself, *This guy really does have possibilities!*

Gary and Joan left for Las Vegas that Friday directly after their classes ended. They checked into their hotel room and Joan felt thoroughly excited in anticipation as Gary helped her undress. He took off his own clothes and Joan felt even more excited as she saw how aroused he was. She opened her arms and pulled him down on top of her. She surrendered completely to the erotic sensations as their bodies merged.

Moments later as they lay together breathing heavily, Joan whispered in Gary's ear, "That was fun." Gary murmured his agreement. They slept for an hour or two. When Joan awoke, she saw Gary staring at her naked body and smiling.

She asked, "What now?"

"Hey, how about an encore?" Gary suggested.

Joan laughed and replied, "I'm game, but how about some food first? I'm famished."

"Okay," said Gary. "I'll tell you what. Let's go downstairs. I'd like to hit the craps table for a few minutes. Have you ever shot dice?"

"No," replied Joan. "Why don't you show me?"

They dressed quickly and headed for the craps tables. Joan could see immediately that Gary was not a beginner. He did quite well and within five minutes he had a growing pile of chips. Meanwhile, a waitress had delivered their drink orders and Gary polished off two martinis. "Say," said Joan. "Remember I told you I'm hungry? Come on, let's eat."

"Okay," replied Gary, who scooped up his chips. Hand in hand, they headed for the restaurant. At dinner, Gary ordered a bottle of red wine and Joan noticed that, except for her one glass, Gary drank it all.

"Isn't that a bit much?" asked Joan. "And you had two drinks before dinner, didn't you?"

"Oh, who's counting," said Gary. "After all, I'm not driving, am I?"

Joan smiled, but thought to herself, *This is something new. I wonder how often he drinks this much.* Then she thought, *Oh, why should I worry? After all, it's our first vacation weekend together. Maybe some celebration is in order.*

After dinner, she and Gary went back to the same craps table. "My lucky table," said Gary. She watched him play and he seemed to do quite well for about a half hour. Then she observed his pile of chips getting smaller and smaller and finally it disappeared altogether. She also noticed he was no longer smiling and that he had another martini.

Finally, he walked away from the table, disconsolate, and said, "I don't know what happened. My luck suddenly went down the tubes and I'm a bit in the hole."

"What do you mean? Do you owe money?" she asked.

"Yeah, I'm about a thousand behind. But I've got two more days. I'll make it up."

Joan wondered about this comment as they walked to the theater to see a well-known comedian perform. "Don't you think you've gambled enough?" asked Joan. "Isn't a thousand dollars behind a good place to call it quits?"

"No way," replied Gary. "I'm going to win it all back!"

Joan smiled but thought, *I wonder about this gambling and drinking. I'd better reread the explanation about the checklist item concerning alcohol and gambling.*

They finally went to bed well after midnight but not before Gary spent another twenty minutes at the craps table where he lost again.

Both were tired as they lay in bed together but very aroused. So before they slept they enjoyed another round of lovemaking.

The next two days went all too quickly, filled with pleasure. Sex was frequent and fulfilling. Joan and Gary enjoyed each other and the only drawbacks that Joan felt were Gary's seeming inability to stay away from the craps table and his drinking.

"Why don't we play some blackjack together?" said Joan. "Then I won't have to just stand around and watch you lose."

"Well, okay," Gary said somewhat reluctantly. After about a half hour at the five dollar blackjack table, Gary was restless. "Look," he said, "come back with me to the craps tables and if I don't start to win, I'll stop and we can do something else— maybe go for a swim."

Joan did not want to play blackjack alone so she said, "Okay, but no more than a half hour."

"Okay," said Gary, "it's a deal!"

So they went back to the craps table. Gary ordered a mar- tini from a waitress, grabbed the dice and within a half hour managed to lose another thousand dollars. It was clear to Joan that he was very depressed at his loss. He ordered still another martini and suggested, "Look, I'm not doing well at the tables today. Let's go back to blackjack; you play and I'll advise you."

"Okay," Joan agreed, "I'll try."

Surprisingly, with Gary's coaching, Joan won $150 at blackjack. "Well," she said, "I'm $150 ahead. I'd like to quit and cash in. I've had enough gambling and I've got an idea for something else for us to do."

"Okay," agreed Gary. "I just wish I had your luck."

Joan cashed in her chips and over lunch she said to Gary, "Look, you're a lot better in bed than you are at the craps table, so let's get into bed now that we've eaten and see if you are luckier in love than you are at the tables."

"Good idea," agreed Gary. Shortly after they were back in their hotel room and undressed. Within minutes they were again locked together in a delicious embrace.

This is amazing. The sex is wonderful, thought Joan as she pulled Gary close. *But,* she worried, *what about his uncontrollable urge to gamble? I'm really falling for him and I just hope his gambling and drinking doesn't screw up our relationship.*

Just as she was falling asleep Joan was aware that Gary was gently shaking her. "Wake up, sweetheart." Joan woke up slowly, cuddled by Gary. They were face-to-face. Gary kissed her; his breath was sweet with only the faintest odor of alcohol. She held him close.

"Sweetheart," Gary murmured, "I've got a question for you."

"What's the question?"

Gary asked, "Will you marry me?"

Joan was surprised and thrilled. She was tempted to say yes. She hesitated and then said, "Gary, I'm glad you asked. I do love you and I know you'd make a great husband and I'd like to say yes right now, but I can't." As she said this, she felt him stiffen and start to pull away. She tightened her arms around him saying, "Let me finish."

Before she could continue, Gary said, "I don't understand. If you do really love me, what's your problem?" He sounded angry and hurt.

Joan replied, "Let me tell you. I'm very worried about your gambling and drinking. I don't think I could live in a marriage where my husband went on weekend gambling binges, losing two or three thousand dollars and drinking the amount of alcohol I saw you consume during these last three days. Can you see my point?"

Gary was silent for a long moment. "Joan, it's only a long weekend in Las Vegas. And maybe I should have left the craps table after I lost the first thousand, but I can't believe you would turn me down just because of a couple of unlucky dice rolls and a few drinks. Come on. Can't you look at this with a more logical perspective?"

"Well," she replied, "I guess it is a matter of perception. Let me put it this way: I want to marry you. I think we would have a terrific life together, but how about giving both of us time to really think this through? Do you love me enough to do this?"

Gary replied, "Of course. I have no intention of letting you get away and letting some other man have you." He moved closer into her embrace and, as their bodies meshed, Joan succumbed to the pure pleasure of their union and was able to temporarily push her doubts to the back of her mind. But still they remained.

The next morning was clear and sunny, a beautiful, warm summer day. As they ate breakfast, Joan tried to take an objective look at Gary, who was smiling as he said, "Sweetheart, I meant what I said last night and I look forward to many happy morning meals just like this one after we're married. And I've been thinking about what you said and I do understand your concern. I'm going to show you I can control my gambling and drinking. You just wait and see."

Joan felt comforted by Gary's promise. She needed this assurance. Ever since awaking, a disturbing refrain had been running through her mind: *I may have made a mistake checking off so many "YES" items for Gary on the checklist, before I started to realize that he may be addicted to gambling or alcohol or both.* And then, seeing him in the morning, so bright, handsome and clean-cut, she felt guilty. She thought, *What am I doing? Maybe this whole Las Vegas gambling and drinking was just temporary aberrant behavior; it may not be the real Gary. Am I being too tough on him?*

As she packed for their return trip, she reconsidered, thinking, *I owe it to myself and to Gary and to our future marriage—if we marry—to be a little more dispassionate and a little less influenced by fun together.* She felt a warm sensation in her pelvic area as she recalled and relived the thrilling sex of the previous night. But, as best she could, she pushed those memories to the back of her mind, took a deep breath and forced herself to think about the checklist, where she had already given Gary "YES" on most of the boxes. She considered item 19: Mature Judgment on which she had already given Gary a "YES." Now she thought, *How can I say Gary has mature judgment if he loses thousands of dollars gambling and won't stop? He must know it's common knowledge that the odds are always with the house and that most gamblers lose. Then there's all the alcohol he consumed.* Joan also wondered about how alcohol might affect his ability to make the decisions required of a good parent, the need to provide guidance for children, to protect them and to make sure they receive good medical care, etc. She also wondered if his gambling might affect their financial security. Joan had heard stories about husbands who gambled away life savings and even mortgaged their homes to pay gambling debts or to finance more attempts to "break the bank." Then her mind swung back to Gary and again she asked herself, *Am I being too hard on him? Are his gambling and drinking really addictions or just "one-time problems" that happened to occur because we were away?* If Gary was an addict, whether to gambling or drinking or both, Joan wondered if it might be genetic and could be inherited.

Then she found herself really becoming anxious and worrying as she thought about another issue that could affect the mature judgment item. She thought, *Might his drinking and gambling, if they persisted, cause him to find reasons to perhaps even leave the marriage after children arrive? Also, would his gambling and drinking affect his conduct in other areas, such as the obligation to be punctual or conscientious about showing up at appointments?* She had heard that people who are on drinking binges let everything "slide." She wondered if drinking might affect his ability to control his anger since she had heard of "mean drunks." So she thought, *I'd better take a good, hard look at the mature judgment question.* She decided to reserve a verdict on item 19 and to also keep an open mind on other checklist items, which she thought she should review carefully.

Answering the checklist questions is not so easy, Joan thought to herself. She wondered if she really knew whether or not Gary was generous. She wondered whether he would just spend money on himself or if he would be serious about his obligation to his wife and children. It also occurred to her that she still did not have any idea why Gary's mother and father divorced. Also, what aspects of his parents' personalities and behaviors had affected Gary? Did he interpret their divorce as a preferred solution for marital conflicts? Would his parents' decision to divorce influence Gary? Would Gary consider a similar decision to separate if conflict occurred between them? Joan was aware of the potential intergenerational effect of such a parental decision.

Joan was encouraged by Gary's telling her of his positive experience with his grandfather with whom he spent part of his summer vacations. Gary had told Joan how he admired the affectionate relationship between his grandparents, something he did not experience with his own parents, and he told Joan he hoped he could provide such an environment for his own family. She hoped that Gary's experience with his grandparents, which extended into his teenage years, would enhance his capacity to commit and sustain a long-term relationship. She was encouraged knowing that he had maintained a positive relationship with his mother, sister and grandparents. Also she noted that he was loyal and sustained his friendships from early childhood. Joan also liked the fact that Gary and she shared the same religion and political affiliation. And she knew from her discussions with Gary that he and she agreed in their desire to have children. So she had no problems putting check marks in the "YES" boxes for these three items.

However, Joan still did not know whether Gary would be able to accept advice or whether he would be flexible in making the many decisions that are involved in family life. She hoped, in the following weeks and months, that she would find answers to these questions.

She also realized that up to this point in their dating, she had never discovered whether Gary had suffered from any major illness or whether he had any major legal problems. She reminded herself to casually bring up these subjects in the near future.

Her final conclusion was that she had better have a long engagement with Gary of at least a year so that she would have an accurate indication of whether or not he would be able to control his gambling and alcohol behavior. She recalled that alcohol and gambling addictions were red flag items that had to be taken very seriously. She also resolved to take a fresh look and reevaluate Gary on the other checklist items. By the time she had mulled over these thoughts, she and Gary were in the car ready to drive home.

Gary looked at her curiously. "Why have you been so quiet? Is anything wrong?" He seemed genuinely concerned.

Impulsively, Joan loosened her seatbelt, leaned over and kissed him firmly on his cheek. "No, sweetheart, everything is great," she said. "But I've been thinking about what we discussed concerning marriage and about what you promised me and about what you are going to do about the gambling and drinking." She saw him stiffen and she put her hand on his shoulder. She said, "Look, I take you at your word and I have confidence you will do as you promised. I'm really looking forward to our life together." Slowly, Gary relaxed and smiled.

Once back in her apartment, Joan reflected on how she had thoroughly enjoyed their few days in Las Vegas, but she remained concerned about Gary's gambling and drinking. Again she thought, *Maybe I overreacted. After all, maybe it was a one-time Las Vegas mistake. I hope so.*

A couple of weeks later, Gary told Joan, "Tomorrow is my regular Friday night poker game and I'd like to introduce you to my poker buddies. Would you come with me? You don't have to stay."

"Sure," Joan agreed.

The next evening after dinner, Gary drove Joan to a friend's apartment where the poker game was just getting started. Joan noticed that there were two full bottles of scotch, one of which was already open, on the table. Gary introduced her to his three friends.

One of them, Jim, said, "We certainly heard a lot about you, but Gary didn't mention he was going out with such a beauty. Would you like to play with us?"

Joan blushed, "Thank you, that's a very nice compliment. But I don't play poker. Why don't you guys get on with your game and I'll come back and pick up Gary a little bit later."

They agreed that Joan would pick up Gary in a couple of hours; Joan left to go back home to her studying. As she drove away she thought to herself, *More gambling and more drinking. They had two bottles of scotch for four guys. What is going on?* Suddenly she remembered the checklist and murmured, "I hope I don't wind up with a 'NO' on checklist item 33," even though that's exactly what she felt compelled to do.

She dutifully picked up Gary after the poker game. He did not seem drunk, but she noticed that his speech was a little slurred. She asked him, "Well, were you a big winner tonight?"

Gary replied, "I wish I could say yes, but I did come out a little behind."

Joan nodded and thought, *I'd better not ask him how much he lost, particularly since I calculate he already lost about two thousand during our trip to Las Vegas.*

They rode in silence for a while. Then Joan said, "Gary, I want to tell you what I'm thinking now, before we jump into bed. As I told you in Las Vegas, I love you and do want to marry you and I'm delighted you feel the same about me. But look at tonight: your regular Friday night poker date. There were two bottles of scotch for four guys when I dropped you off. And when I picked you up, I noticed that most of the scotch was gone. I don't know how much you drank, but I do know you gambled tonight and lost money, as you just told me. I've done some reading and I hope you agree with me that you certainly give the perception of someone who has a real gambling and drinking problem—maybe not a big and insoluble problem, but a problem nonetheless. What do you think?"

Gary was silent as he sat in the car, now stopped outside of his apartment. He opened his mouth as if to speak, but he closed it, still silent. He seemed miserable. Joan felt she had to go on, "Do you love me enough to promise, really promise, that you will get help if you need it and you'll give up gambling and drinking, because these are two habits that really worry me."

Gary stared at Joan. He seemed to be in a state of shock. "You mean you love me, but you think I'm really an alcoholic and a gambler?"

Joan said, "Well, what do you think? It's not only what happened in Las Vegas and how much you lost there, but now I see something I didn't know about during the time we've been together. You gamble every Friday night and drink with your buddies. I'm worried about your drinking so much. And the gambling too."

"Well, you know," said Gary, "as I told you when we were in Las Vegas, it's a matter of how you look at it. And I guess when you put it all together—what happened in Las Vegas and now my Friday night playing poker with my friends—I really do understand how it must look and I admit you've got a point. But I've been playing poker with these friends for a long time. I admit that we do drink more than we should. And I'm not proud about my behavior in Las Vegas."

Joan waited before she replied: "I thought you would own up and face the problem and I'm glad you did. I will say that I feel, in every other way that I can tell so far, that you and I are made for each other. If you really put some limits on drinking and gambling—and I hope you can—I know we can have a wonderful life together. But let's not announce our engagement yet. I think we should let some time go by. Frankly, it will give me a chance to feel more comfortable about your decision to kick your gambling and drinking habit. I want to be sure you're comfortable about it, because if you're not and if it's going to bother you, then things are not going to work well between us. On the other hand, if we're dating and seeing each other regularly, our relationship will deepen and we will both be more secure in our decision to marry. So let's delay our engagement five or six months."

Gary smiled, "You've got a deal." Joan moved into his waiting arms, smiling and crying at the same time.

GARY AND JOAN'S FUTURE

We will leave Gary and Joan at this point in their relationship. Joan is wise to spend more time developing their relationship, although it seems clear that these two plan to get married. Regular and exclusive dating will give Joan an opportunity to see if Gary's promise to give up gambling and control his drinking is fulfilled. Time will provide Joan with the opportunity to determine if Gary is serious about modifying his behavior.

Joan is quite conscious of the serious problems in the relationship posed by these red flag items but hopeful that Gary will come through so that they can marry. Only time will tell if Gary is actually able to fulfill his promises about controlling these potential addictions.

In this chapter we have viewed a new scenario for Gary and Joan, one in which Joan used the checklist to help her evaluate the relationship. If she continues to refer to the checklist, she will have help deciding how to answer Gary's proposal. Utilizing the checklist, her own insight and strength to face potential problems, we believe she will be able to constructively handle the issues and assist Gary in modifying his addictive behavior.

It is also true that a successful relationship will depend on Gary's acknowledging and dealing with his problem. Promises are usually not enough. To modify his drinking and gambling, Gary may need to seek either individual or group support.

Joan didn't have to come to the decision she did in our reconfigured story. She could have ended the relationship, but since she felt that, in every other way, they were well matched, she decided he was a potential spouse she did not want to "let get away." Nevertheless, having come to the conclusion that she wants to make the relationship work, she remains well aware of the fact that these addictions are not easy to eliminate, so we feel that she is wise to wait a good amount of time before making a decision to marry. If all is well at that point, she and Gary can enter into a formal engagement and then finally get married.

Our second rendition of the Gary and Joan story also illustrates how Joan was able to inject some rational and logical thinking into the romance despite their intense, continuing and mutually enjoyable sex life. It is not very easy for a partner to maintain some perspective, as Joan did, given the tremendously enjoyable chemistry that the couple enjoyed. After all, it was clear that Joan and Gary had developed a close relationship. They had much in common. Many positive attributes were noted. There was agreement on most of the important issues and they shared many mutual elements of companionship. They enjoyed spending time together; their attachment was far more than sexual.

It is important to recognize that marriage and Gary's affection for Joan will not cure Gary of his problems. Many partners enter marriage feeling that as loving mates they can change their spouses' behavior and cure their difficulties. In reality many of the stresses faced in the early years of marriage often increase the negative behavior of one partner.

In the months to come, Joan will be able to evaluate Gary and to make an informed decision about entering marriage with him.

chapter five

Using Dating, Courtship and Engagement as Learning Periods

The sooner in a potentially serious relationship one uses the checklist the better, because a bond may begin to form early in the dating process. As feelings and emotions grow they often can cloud the ability to make a rational evaluation of a prospective spouse. When the connection progresses, the parties usually develop mutual empathy and consideration for each other's feelings as well as the desire for more proximity and contact. Intense emotions may override good judgments that might otherwise cause one partner to end the relationship.

It can be increasingly difficult to separate from a developing attachment figure. Often, the prospect of being alone, without contact, companionship or sexual pleasure can be more anxiety provoking and frightening than continuing a dysfunctional relationship. This is similar to the feelings of a child who is physically and emotionally abused by a parent but will often elect to remain with that well known and familiar parent rather than be removed from the destructive environment and placed in a safe but strange, unknown institutional haven or foster home.

When couples continue to date and become better acquainted, it is not difficult to understand how the partners can become attached to one another. Depending upon the couple and the circumstances of the relationship, such a bond can become very intense, making a breakup difficult. Therefore, as explained by Parkes and Stevenson-Hinde in *The Place of Attachment in Human Behavior,* the threatened loss of such an attachment figure is associated with feelings of "abandonment."[1] In addition, John Bowlby explains in *Loss* how couples can be "kept together for long periods by an intense and shared fear of loneliness."[2]

An individual may also be reluctant to end a relationship because of concern for the feelings of the partner, particularly if he or she has experienced other previous rejections. In addition, there may be a tendency to continue an unwise relationship to avoid giving pain to the other person.

The story of Jonathan and Anna illustrates how difficult it may be to sever a developing attachment.

After a few months of dating, Jonathan realized that Anna was moody, depressed and, at times, dysfunctional. Even though he was physically attracted to her, he realized that they were not well suited. Jonathan was kind and empathetic and thought that he could change Anna and rescue her from her moods. He was reluctant to inflict more pain on Anna, who had many early losses. In the end they stayed together, but neither found joy in their relationship.

Breaking up a relationship may also be more difficult if there are fewer alternative choices available in the marital "pool," i.e., if your pool of prospective spouses is small, you may be less likely to voluntarily separate and end a relationship (more on this in chapter 6). If you have many choices from available prospects, this will increase your confidence to rationally evaluate those whom you meet. You will find it easier to opt out of a relationship if more prospects are "waiting in the wings."

Any separation from an ongoing relationship will often evoke emotions of anger, depression or sadness. Rejection is usually stressful and painful both for the victim and the one breaking the relationship. This is especially true if one or both have experienced early traumas involving the loss of or separation from a parent or primary caregiver, teenage rejection from peers or a failed adult love affair. Resolving these feelings can take time—sometimes considerable amounts of time—before a person returns to emotional equilibrium, particularly if the couple was intimate.

As we've indicated, the separation process itself may be more painful than continuing the unwise relationship. For many, a questionable relationship is better than none at all.

In our second Joan/Gary example, Joan became aware of Gary's gambling and alcohol addictions, but she was reluctant to break up with him, because she had become emotionally attached and had grown to love him. Had Joan known of these addictions in the very beginning, before she and Gary became so bonded, she may have felt more willing to end the relationship and look elsewhere, thus avoiding the emotional stress of separation. Or if she chose to remain in the relationship with Gary, she may have been more prepared to deal with problems that might have developed because of his addictions. So it is important, as early as possible in the relationship, to recognize negative qualities in a potential spouse and decide whether or not you can live with them before an attachment is formed. It is emotionally less painful and much easier to do this earlier rather than later in the dating and courtship period.

However, as shown in the story of Joan and Gary, many negative characteristics may not be apparent in the early stages of dating and courtship. Several reasons contribute to the late discovery of negative traits and behavior:

- During the initial dating period, both partners are often on their best behavior and, unconsciously or otherwise, conceal their more primitive and negative conduct.
- Many couples may not engage in enough different kinds of activities or discussions over a long enough period of time for negative qualities to be revealed and allow for a more accurate

evaluation. A long period of dating, courtship and engagement will provide the time and opportunity for more activities, which will aid in the formation of a realistic evaluation.

- Persons who are searching for a close relationship may not recognize or choose to ignore warning signs. They may hope unrealistically that undesirable behavior will be modified and that "love will find a way."

Loretta and Bill are a couple who experienced relationship conflicts because of their secrets.

Loretta and Bill had dated for several months and enjoyed their time together. They had become sexually intimate and Bill thought they had real possibilities as a couple. But their contact together was primarily going to dinner and a movie followed by very satisfactory sex and only an occasional overnight.

They were very close to becoming engaged. Yet each had some significant problems of which the other was completely unaware. Bill had a serious heart problem that might require disabling surgery. He did not want Loretta to know about it. He knew she would be distressed and was concerned that this information might influence their relationship. Loretta also had secrets, primarily her mounting credit card debt, over $10,000 and climbing. She could not seem to control her buying binges. If she saw a sale or a bargain, she took out her credit card and charged the items she coveted. She was only paying the minimum required by the credit card company. Her payments were mostly high interest, which she knew was increasing as was her unpaid balance. She did not want Bill to know anything about this, because she felt that it could endanger their relationship.

Loretta and Bill's issues demonstrate how secrets can be a source of stress and future conflict. If Loretta and Bill had spent more time together talking about themselves and engaged in more varied activities, these problems may have surfaced earlier in the courtship. Planning a trip to the beach or a park, shopping, visiting a family member or having friends over for an evening would also provide a different insight into the behaviors and attitudes of a potential mate. If these two decide to live together, such intimate and sustained togetherness will raise the odds that these issues will be exposed. It will help them to avoid an unwise early marriage. In the end, Bill's medical issues and Loretta's compulsive spending will probably be disclosed. She may notice him taking medications. He will see her bills piling up. At some point this couple must decide how they will deal with these problems and whether to continue their relationship despite these issues.

Should Loretta and Bill make the decision to live together? Let's consider the pros and cons of this option.

DECIDING TO LIVE TOGETHER

There are conflicting views in various studies and articles about the advisability and consequences of living together before marriage. Some state that cohabiting favors the odds of successful marriage while others reach the opposite conclusion. We feel that logic supports our view: premarital cohabitation can be a very positive and revealing experience since it provides a couple the opportunity to test the marital environment to see if it "feels right." Without doubt, partners learn more about each other if they share living quarters, eat and sleep together, use the same bathroom, pay bills, clean and cook together. Usually they will spend their evenings and weekends with each other, even if they both have full-time jobs. There will be opportunities for observation of temperaments and their abilities to nurture and occasions to gain information about their family histories and relationships. Although he does not approve of cohabitation, therapist and author Jeffry Larson in *Should We Stay Together?*[3] concedes that the negative effects of cohabitation are less if the couple plans to marry. We firmly believe that cohabitation should only take place between couples with a definite or at least tentative decision to marry.

For some couples there may be religious or family issues that would foreclose the option of living together. They may not experience the described advantages of shared living and the information it would reveal. Nevertheless, even without living together, a long courtship or engagement should produce the necessary information to make an informed decision on the prospective spouse.

WHEN NOT TO LIVE TOGETHER

We strongly recommend that couples *not* live together until they have had the opportunity to experience an extended courtship and have decided that they are a good match for each other and that each is able to fulfill the four spousal roles. Most importantly, they should not move in together until they have made either a tentative or definite decision to marry. Unfortunately, many couples decide, quite casually, that they will share an apartment or room and move in together to save money or for other reasons. Usually, they have not decided to marry and give little, if any, thought to the potentially dangerous consequences of their casual decision. Many focus on the convenience and availability of regular sex plus newly acquired household economies.

There is almost no consideration in current literature that even mentions the obvious and most negative result of cohabitation: it signals to everyone that both the male and female involved are "out of circulation" and unavailable for other relationships. Deciding to live together causes spouse seekers to bypass the very essential period of dating and courtship, during which they have the opportunity to evaluate more than one prospect. It locks them together into a closed relationship. Few spouse seekers would date a man or woman who is living with someone. As the partners live together, with sexual and financial ties, sharing food, rent and other expenses, their external social relationships are drastically altered. Their living together sends the community a message: "We are exclusive, are not available and are no longer playing the field." They are far less likely to break up, regardless of provocations. Since both are "out of circulation"—perhaps for an extended period of time—they may feel reluctant to reenter the dating scene. Furthermore, if one or both of the partners feel that things are not going well and if a breakup is considered, there is another factor (aside from inertia) that will tend to keep the couple together, perhaps in an unwise relationship. At least one of them will need to search for, find and arrange to live elsewhere, which may require the expenditure of considerable time and money (buying furniture, supplies, etc.) So, consciously or otherwise, some couples will conclude that it is easier to stay together. Many slide into unwise marriages.

We believe there is a better and safer approach for partners who feel they are in a promising relationship and who have reached a decision, definite or tentative, that they will marry. They should both retain their own living quarters and try out the living together option for a month or two (or more). Then, if warning signs appear, it is easy to split, move back to the retained living quarters and resume the process of searching and dating.

COURTSHIP AS A DISCOVERY PERIOD

The dating and courtship period, if it is long enough and if it provides frequent contact, should offer ample opportunity to consider all the items on the checklist. The checklist should be used as a guide that can be examined at various times over the weeks and months of dating. There are no right or wrong answers. Furthermore, answers can be changed as each individual becomes better known to the other.

The pluses of taking time to get to know each other are portrayed by Edna and Al's relationship.

Edna had some real doubts about Al, whom she had been dating for about two months. She felt he was somewhat depressed and dour, even though she knew that he was very bright. But one day, when they went sailing alone on his boat, she saw another side to Al. On that occasion he seemed full of fun and energy and was very upbeat. In time, as the dating progressed, she realized she had been quite wrong in her earlier assessment as she learned to know other aspects of his personality, so she corrected item 17: Cheerful from a "NO" to a "YES."

The Edna/Al example demonstrates the importance of using a prolonged courtship period to engage in a variety of activities that reveal different facets of partners' personalities. It was several months before Edna had the opportunity to observe Al in a different physical setting. Only then did she realize that she had been mistaken in concluding he was depressed and moody. Every couple should vary their activities and social situations so that over time they can more accurately evaluate their potential spouses.

During this period each spouse prospect can explore the checklist and decide whether the positive items are sufficient to trump the negative qualities of the future mate. Each can evaluate whether or not he or she can live with some of the negatives aspects of the other. It is best that both members of the couple are aware of and use the rating and evaluation process or that at least one of them has the knowledge and insight to make the "YES" or "NO" responses. Remember: the checklist applies to *both* spouse seekers!

With some couples, only one member may be aware of the checklist and its items. For example, in our second Joan and Gary example (chapter 4), it doesn't appear Joan ever told Gary about her checklist evaluations. Hopefully at some point she will, as it would probably be a wise move on her part. After all, no one is perfect and she and Gary should be mature enough to discuss both the positives and negatives of their relationship. Such full disclosure and discussions, including those concerning Gary's addictions and any other possible issues, should enhance the prospects for a successful marriage.

There is enormous variation in the types of behavior that an individual can tolerate. Couples will need to answer these questions: Can both of us live with the concept that "no one is perfect"? Will we each be willing, for the long term, to accept and live with the behaviors and disabilities (if any) of the other?

DETERMINE NURTURING ABILITY

Whether or not you choose to live together, remember that this period of time presents you with your only opportunity before marriage to determine how well you and your partner will fulfill two of the four roles required of every spouse. We are referring to the roles of Friend/Companion/Advisor and of Lover (discussed in chapter 3). During courtship, we strongly suggest that every couple ask themselves some specific questions that can be very helpful in foretelling whether their relationship can be sustained and will flourish. These very important questions involve and test the capacity of the couple to nurture each other during all of the marital years.

The Nurturing Checklist

1. Have I or my partner said something positive, complimentary or supporting today?
2. Have we both been responsive to our mutual needs for help, such as taking on specific chores or otherwise assisting the other person?
3. Have we listened to each other when one of us was upset, concerned or not well and acknowledged the current problem?
4. Have we been responsive to the other's need for food, rest and protection?
5. If one or both of us are angry, upset or irritated, do we pick an appropriate time to discuss the issue when both partners have "cooled down"?
6. Do we communicate non-verbal affection by holding, hugging, kissing and caressing?

7. Are we reasonably flexible in agreeing to sex when one of us desires it?

Responses to these nurturing questions will definitely help to clarify many of the checklist items, since our answers provide information about the compatibility of each partner in many important and very personal day-to-day activities.

In our next case history we discuss Leona and Ed's problems after becoming engaged and moving in together.

After an intensive five-month courtship, Leona accepted Ed's marriage proposal. Ed suggested that they set a marriage date but Leona deferred. She had been badly hurt in a previous relationship and told Ed, "Let's not rush. First let's see how we get along and then we can decide on our wedding date." Ed happily moved into Leona's apartment.

Privately, Leona thought, *I feel in my heart that Ed is the man for me, but for both our sakes I want to be sure. And after some time—maybe weeks or maybe months—I'll feel more comfortable with planning for our wedding.* Leona was also concerned about how she should answer the checklist item on sexual attraction. While she felt that she and Ed had great sex together, she was concerned, because Ed wanted sex almost every single day and she felt it was just too much. She felt badgered to the point that it was beginning to upset her. She wondered if perhaps they were not sexually compatible. So on their first night together in bed after Ed moved in, she decided to broach the subject. She took a deep breath and said, "Sweetheart, I enjoy our sex. It's great and I look forward to it, but can't we slow down our love life to two or three times a week?"

Ed looked shocked. "Sweetheart, why didn't you say something before? Of course we can slow down; after all, we have many years ahead and plenty of time. I just thought that you wanted us to make love every day."

Leona sighed with relief, hugged Ed and said, "That's why I adore you. I should have mentioned my concern before; I'm sorry I didn't. We're going to have a great life together."

Ed's response to this sexual issue is an example of his flexibility and willingness to listen. Leona was also able to bring up her dissatisfaction at an appropriate time when both were able to communicate with warmth and understanding. It is not always easy to share one's feelings, especially those dealing with sexual matters, but partners need to let each other know their feelings and desires so that they build a mutually fulfilling relationship.

TIMETABLE FOR COURTSHIP AND ENGAGEMENT

We strongly advise against a *whirlwind courtship* and quick marriage. Many would agree with the proposition that male and female should become well acquainted before entering into marriage. Research tells us that many couples who "knew" it was "love at first sight" and married within weeks or a few months have experiences similar to Joan and Gary's first example and with the same disastrous consequences. Love at first sight can occur, but it takes time and varied experiences together to test and evaluate the enduring quality of that emotion. Be aware that love at first sight can be just that. It is prudent and very advisable to take the ample amount of time required to make sure that the love and affection is real and enduring.

Therapist Jeffry Larson suggests a period of at least a year, whether or not there is a formal engagement.[4] We agree and feel that a minimum of six months to a year or even more is advisable for the period of courtship and engagement, with lots of time spent together engaging in all sorts of activities: sports, discussions, parties, vacations, book groups, etc. This will provide the couple with sufficient time to explore the various items indicated in our checklist. If the couple lives together, after carefully considering this important step, it will provide them with information that will be helpful in making the ultimate decision to marry or not. A long period of courtship will provide an increased opportunity to see how your prospective spouse conducts himself or herself in many different social and work situations and how he or she speaks and acts in a group. For example, in social situations, parties or other groups, are you embarrassed by your prospective spouse? Are you proud of him or her? Is there mutual respect? Or are there some behaviors from which problems develop? Don't forget to consider the very real caveats of living together that were previously discussed in this chapter.

But whether or not there is a decision to live together, the courtship/engagement period is essential and should be respected. It provides a mutual opportunity to answer the important questions embodied in our spouse checklist. Joan and Gary's example as well as Warren and Genevieve's (chapter 3) explore these complex issues.

We recognize that our suggested checklist may sound clinical and perhaps a bit unromantic. You may ask: "How can we reduce love and marriage to thirty-five 'YES' or 'NO' boxes?" But our research, our counseling experience and our own long marriage support this more rational approach to the institution of marriage. Perhaps the best argument in favor of our checklist approach is that the present and generally used decision-making process does not work for many couples. If it did, we would not have today's unacceptably high divorce rate. Journalist Caitlin Flanagan discusses the dangerous deterioration of marriage in her *Time* article "Is There Hope for the American Marriage?", pointing out, "There is no other single force causing as much measurable hardship and human misery in this country as the collapse of marriage."[5]

THE NO PREGNANCY WARNING

Finally, when you do tie the knot, it is important to try to plan *no pregnancy* for at least a year. The early period of marriage calls for adjustments: mental, physical, financial and emotional. All of these possibly negative concerns can be ameliorated if pregnancy is delayed until the marriage seems stable and prepared for the very considerable impact of children on the relationship.

Once children arrive, their need for two parents becomes paramount for many reasons. Divorce is usually very stressful for children and can inflict lifetime emotional damage on them (see discussion of checklist item 11). Furthermore, divorce produces increased financial obligations as well as potentially troublesome and painful issues involving custody, child visitation and child support.

chapter six

Searching
for a Spouse

The prospective spouse evaluation process actually begins at the couple's very first contact. We strongly believe that both men and women can and should make good use of their initial contact by beginning to utilize our checklist at this crucial point. Sometimes this is before a man and woman have ever seen one another and even before their first date. Often it begins during the first telephone call between the couple or when they connect on the Internet (as we discuss later in this chapter). Note in our example how Ollie utilized the Prospective Spouse Checklist as he searched for a possible mate.

Ollie was an accountant in his thirties who hoped to meet an attractive young woman to date and someday marry. He was looking for a woman in his age bracket who was a college graduate and whose intelligence was roughly equivalent to his own. He also hoped that his future wife would be able to fulfill the four essential spouse roles: a cooperative, willing sex partner, a good companion, a good mother and a good money manager.

One day, his boss mentioned that he met a "real beauty" whom Ollie might like to date. He gave him Elinor's telephone number. Later that evening, with a feeling of anticipation, Ollie called her. After introducing himself and telling her how he obtained her telephone number, he explained that he'd just moved back to his hometown after working at an out-of-state firm for three years.

He told her, "I'm in my mid-thirties, single, a CPA and like to play golf and hike. Tell me about you."

She seemed friendly and receptive and said, "I am now working in sales at a dress shop downtown part time, but what I really enjoy is singing on weekends when my fifteen-month-old is with her father. One day I hope to be in show business."

They chatted for a while exploring what schools they attended and whether or not they had mutual friends. Ollie did not ask Elinor for a date.

During their first phone call, Ollie discovered that Elinor had a child. Ollie, who has spent time analyzing his own needs and thinking about the qualities and background he wanted in a prospective spouse, had previously decided that a major goal for him in marriage was starting his own family and not beginning marriage as a stepfather. He checked "NO" under item 2: No Children and didn't consider the other items in view of this response. Ollie will continue his search for a more promising prospect who satisfies what he has decided are his goals. Let's now discuss the large number of possible mates available (Ollie's and your potential pools) and how this will help locate an enduring relationship.

A POOL OF SPOUSE PROSPECTS

You may wonder: *Why do I even need a pool?* We feel you will have the opportunity to make a much wiser choice if you have more possible mates from which to choose. Martha, a young woman who lived over a hundred years ago, is an example of someone who had limited prospective partners. Let's briefly consider what choice used to mean in the past and what it means today.

In 1889, Martha, in her twenties, lived on a family farm. Martha was thinking about marriage. There were three nearby farms where the families were large, but there was only one young man of marrying age in each family. There was also a small town nearby in which there were dances once a month and Martha had hoped that she might meet someone attractive at one of these functions. But her experiences at these dances had not been very promising. Martha liked to read and had other intellectual pursuits. She was hoping that she might meet a man who shared these interests. She also hoped that she might find a partner who would be hardworking, interesting and a stimulating companion. But so far she had not had much luck and had little hope that her Prince Charming would come to the farm.

Martha shares the lament of many spouse seekers of both sexes who complain, "I can't seem to meet any decent prospects" or "The good ones are already married. If they are available they are divorced and have children" or "I have met some terrific people, but the most attractive ones are not interested in me."

Martha's problem is classic. Because of her location on a rural farm, her choice of possible suitors was limited. Because she was needed on the farm to help with the chores and had to care for her sick mother, she could not move to a city. Unless she was very lucky, she would have to settle for one of the young men whom she had met on nearby farms or the few other young men whom she had met at the monthly dances. Unfortunately, she did not find any of them very interesting or attractive. She yearned to meet a man with whom she could enjoy a real romance.

Her story underscores the basic problem of choice, which exists any time we must make a decision among alternatives, whether it is what we eat, what clothes to wear or what social functions to attend. Martha would have been in a far better position if she had the opportunity to select a possible suitor from many eligible men instead of only seven or eight. Then she could have attempted to become acquainted with a variety of young men with similar interests and found someone who shared her pastimes. It is unfortunate for Martha that she was not searching in the computer era, because today's world offers men like Ollie and women like Martha a much larger choice of mates.

Today, men and women either live in or near large cities or are able to make contact on the computer with many eligible individuals. We will now examine these third millennium men and women and discover who they are and how easily they connect.

POSSIBLE MATE POOL

Demographics in the United States and other countries have changed, taking millions of people from widely scattered farms and placing them in cities. Here they are thrown together daily in apartments, elevators, automobiles, buses, subways, business establishments, recreation locales, etc. Such close contact along with largely absent traditional barriers combine to create a broad and deep pool of potential spouses.

Males and females can now easily communicate with many eligible members of the opposite sex. This is done by all types of methods: computers, traditional telephones, cell phones, etc. Except for the telephone, these devices, in usable and affordable form, have only been in existence in recent years.

The breakdown and virtual elimination of class barriers, particularly in Western democracies like the United States (and elsewhere), further increases choice. Today in many Western cultures, class prohibitions have diminished if not disappeared entirely. The old racial, cultural, language and religious barriers are coming down. So are social and economic barriers, resulting in far more social and economic mobility. The available mate pool is enlarging.

Penniless high school graduates with parents subsisting on food stamps may win scholarships and end up at Ivy League colleges, which will further expand their opportunities to locate suitable spouses. A student may even reach foreign shores on a Rhodes Scholarship. Or a young man whose parents were a multiracial couple, the father from Kenya and the mother an American divorcee, who was raised by a grandmother in Hawaii, becomes a Harvard-educated lawyer. These poor boys may become wealthy, educated and admired—and even become president!

HOW TO USE YOUR POOL
Let's determine how you, the spouse seeker, can search among this multitude of eligible men and women. We'll explore how you can learn to pick and choose between those who are desirable and those who are not. If one possible mate does not appear to suit you, you can terminate that relationship and move on as promptly as possible to another more desirable prospect who is available from the pool. As you become more adept at contacting potential mates and making decisions about possible choices, you will find the whole process less threatening. Trolling the Internet, where you can quickly and easily "interview" scores of eligible people, can be interesting and enjoyable. Now let's explore how you can easily access and "work" the pool to aid in your search for Mr. or Ms. Right. We will examine each group and element in the pool and explore how best to use them.

FAMILY, FRIENDS AND RELATIVES AS SOURCES
People you know are your best resource for a potential spouse. Most of us need help in many activities involving interaction with others, particularly in searching for a spouse. It is only logical therefore, in a spouse search, to add to your own personal efforts by enlisting the help of those who know you, care about you and are interested in you. This means your family, friends and relatives. Most family members, friends and relatives will almost automatically screen prospects for you. If, for example, your aunt happens to mention a possible marital prospect, she will probably communicate to you her honest

perceptions concerning attractiveness, height, weight, etc. Psychologist Dr. Joy Browne, in the book *Dating for Dummies*, agrees with us in this regard: Friends and relatives are good sources for dating and spouse possibilities. Dr. Browne also includes an additional source: ex-husbands or ex-wives.[1] In selected cases, we agree that this interesting suggestion is worth consideration.

To take advantage of your family members', friends' and relatives' contacts, you must organize yourself and you must be persistent. Make a list including telephone numbers of all friends and relatives whom you would be comfortable calling. It is understandable if you feel somewhat squeamish in asking friends and relatives to help you locate prospective dates, just the way many salespersons probably feel when they are required to make cold calls to new customers. But the reward for such persistence can certainly be worth the effort. So concentrate on the rewards. Each time you are able to ask a family member or a friend to help find someone eligible for you, you may be moving closer to the time when you locate your future spouse.

To most effectively use your network of family and friends, it is important to remind them regularly. Let's suppose one of your relatives, Uncle Joe, is a business executive. You could mention to Uncle Joe: "I know your company is about fifty-fifty male and female. So how about keeping your eyes open for an eligible guy and see if you can get him to call me?"

This same mind-set—regular and repeated communication with family and friends—can be applied to the many other groups, clubs and activities in which your friends or relatives may be active. A good general rule is to speak to and remind family and friends at least every few months. Note on your calendar: "Call family and friends about prospects."

But how can you find and meet a prospect if there are no family members or friends available or if you have moved to a different location? There are, in fact, several methods that you can use.

MATCHMAKERS: FORMAL AND INFORMAL

Many years before anyone dreamed of the Internet, matchmakers were busy putting males and females together in the United States and other countries throughout the world. Even today there are many personal service organizations as well as individuals that perform the matchmaker function. Since modern matchmakers do not know you, they obtain information and then furnish a list or arrange an initial meeting between candidates they feel will be compatible. To locate these matchmakers, perform an Internet search for matchmaker businesses in your city or look in the phone book under "dating" or "dating services."

On the Internet there are many Web sites that perform matchmaker services to screen and connect candidates. It's Just Lunch is a national organization that, for a small fee, will find you an apparently compatible opposite sex lunch companion who may have long-term possibilities. There are hundreds of similar services and online matchmakers: among them are Matchmaker.com, eHarmony.com and Match.com. They collect information from others like you who are in the market for a spouse and pair up possible matches. All that you need to do is submit some basic information about yourself (age, location, etc.) and pay their fee.

SOCIAL, EDUCATIONAL AND OTHER ONGOING GROUPS

Other options for meeting prospective mates are various groups and activities. Some are organized and scheduled, such as book clubs, cooking classes, dog training groups, dancing classes, educational classes, computer classes, exercise classes, singles groups at religious institutions and many more. Communities of all sizes have many group activities at libraries, schools, churches and synagogues. Look carefully into a group before you make any commitment and especially before you sign any contracts that obligate you financially. Assure yourself in advance that there are enough eligible singles attending. The general rule to follow is to first go and observe before you sign up. Do not accept any "sales pitches" advertising to join unless you personally see that the group has the desired mix, ages and socioeconomic composition with which you will feel comfortable.

If you enjoy reading, consider one of the many book groups that meet at public libraries, schools, etc. Or if you are a dog lover, there are dog parks and training groups where dog owners congregate and meet regularly. Country clubs, golf and tennis clubs and other sports sites are places to check if there are sufficient numbers of prospective dates. Hiking, gardening and nature groups like the Sierra Club may also be of interest. Even if there is not an equal proportion of men and women in a particular group, increasing your circle of friends and acquaintances will allow you the possibilities of other referrals from these new contacts.

Do not forget, with all these groups, to take a good, hard look by going to the meeting place on a trial run for perhaps a few weeks or even a month to make sure you are joining a group where you will have the opportunity to meet other singles in your age range and you will feel socially and intellectually compatible.

Suzy, one woman who was looking for a prospective spouse, moved away from her hometown.

Suzy was a forty-year-old single lawyer. She'd accepted a position with a law firm in a distant city and heard about an upscale health club. On her evening visit to the club, though she was impressed with the high-tech décor and the latest equipment, she observed that all the men seemed to be very good looking although very young. She did not see anyone who appeared to be older than their twenties. She spoke to one of the members who explained that the club was very popular with recent college graduates from a nearby university. She decided to look elsewhere and found a health club in a suburban section of the city with members her own age and some attractive men.

Unorganized locales, such as bars and restaurants, may be where single office workers and professionals look for meeting opportunities before heading home after the workday. The same investigation caveat applies to these informal social sites. Be sure you don't accept other people's views without making a personal visit. Edgar was a single man who employed this to his satisfaction.

Edgar was a lawyer employed by a large downtown Los Angeles law firm. The high-rise office building housing his firm had a very attractive bar and restaurant at ground level and by 6:00 P.M. each workday it was jammed with young men and women in his age group. Although Edgar was very shy, after a few weeks of dropping in for a drink, he felt more comfortable engaging in conversation. He was helped in this endeavor by another young lawyer named Bob who had met his fiancée at the very same restaurant. Bob and his fiancée took Edgar "under their wings" and introduced him to several single women. One of them, Sofia, seemed to be interesting and appealing, with long-range possibilities.

AVOID ONE-SHOT ENCOUNTERS

Vacations and cruises in exotic spots can be interesting and exciting. Weekend self-exploration seminars and retreats can also be stimulating. But none of these "intense encounter" activities are recommended as ideal for men and women intent on finding mates. Our reasoning: Although these one-shot events may allow you to meet someone interesting, they do not provide the repeated and ongoing contact so essential to creating a lasting relationship.

Darcy, one young woman to whom we spoke, is an example of someone who wanted to find a prospective spouse but was looking in the wrong places.

Darcy and her friend Bette signed up for an expensive ten-day Caribbean cruise with top-notch accommodations. The food was great and the singles mixers were fun. Both women met very eligible men on the first days of the cruise and had shipboard romances. However, the men worked in cities that were distant from Darcy and Bette's hometown. Although the four of them talked about a possible reunion, nothing specific was arranged. Darcy was disappointed and realized that she would probably never again see the young man to whom she was attracted.

From our perspective on the spouse hunt, we suggest that you spend your money, energy and time on groups where you can see the same people at least once a week or a few times a month. This sensible approach will facilitate and expedite your search for Mr. or Ms. Right.

OTHER EDUCATION AND TRAINING OPPORTUNITIES

One good opportunity for a young man or woman to find a future husband or wife is during the later years of college, graduate school or some other special training, such as university extension courses, computer courses, writing courses, etc. The men and women in these categories usually have had a few years of experience and have had love interests, dated and gone through breakups. They have had opportunities to experiment with a variety of relationships. They will also have developed some ability to evaluate the personalities, values and characters of those whom they meet and date.[2] Some may have, intuitively, considered many of the items contained in our checklist. By their middle to late twenties, many are ready to take on the task of spouse selection.

Academic environments are excellent places to locate a spouse, because they usually provide an ample period of time, often a year or longer, where there are usually a number of unattached men and women and the quality of the prospects is good. If someone is in college, graduate school or an advanced training or education program, they generally have more than average intelligence. And if they don't already have ample assets or income, they are likely to obtain the training or education in the future to earn an adequate income. Another plus is the fact that such settings usually provide a large pool of unattached prospects, especially if the college or other program is at a larger institution. A final and quite essential point is the need to attend a college where there is a good quantity of both sexes. Fortunately, in today's world, most of the law schools, medical schools, schools of social work or psychology and even some religious seminaries have roughly equivalent numbers of men and women.

During the months or years of attendance at the institutions or in the programs we have considered, both sexes will have the valuable continuing opportunity to learn to know each other in both formal and informal settings. The luxury of unhurried time to mingle will promote discussions of all sorts of topics, whether associated with a learning curriculum or not. In a relaxed atmosphere with student friends, prospective spouse seekers will find and learn to know those with whom they have common interests and are simpatico. They will have the added advantage of being able not only to meet a large group of possibly eligible spouse prospects, but also to quickly discard one unsuitable possibility and move on to someone else. There will be no need to take a large amount of time, which may be required in future years, to locate and meet someone who may be eligible and to move through the months of dating during evenings and weekends. Dating outside of educational environments requires juggling different work schedules. Compare such an arduous looking-flirting-dating scene with the comfort and ease of sitting next to a Mr. or Ms. Eligible during school/class years, day after day, with the opportunity to go for a coffee break between classes, mixed study groups on evenings and weekends, etc. Keep your eyes open if you are in college, graduate school or an equivalent educational program.

Apart from college, graduate school, extension classes and special courses, there are many equivalent spouse search opportunities that are available throughout the United States in all communities, from small towns to cities with millions: writer training/discussion groups, book reading clubs, cooking training and many kinds of seminars. Remember, as mentioned earlier, to attend groups that last at least a few weeks or even months, since it is difficult to do much useful spouse searching on a three-day weekend, no matter how "intense and personal."

Wherever you go and whatever course, college or program you attend, use your Prospective Spouse Checklist. Once you have studied it carefully along with the explanations we have provided, you should be able, during a first date, to consider many of the items and later to answer these questions: Does he or she have long-term possibilities? Should we go out again? Be aware that this will require you and your prospect to explore issues that go beyond cocktail talk and superficial conversation. You will find that dating will be much more interesting and informative if you train yourself to do the kind of conversational "digging" needed to utilize "checklist intelligence."

Let's next look at the "high tech" method of finding a spouse. In this third millennium, it undoubtedly expands the prospective spouse pool a thousand-fold if you use it properly!

INTERNET DATING

Prior to the availability of the Internet, many spouse seekers, especially women, were limited in their pools of prospective partners. The Internet allows seekers to proactively look for and contact prospective spouses. Therefore, we conclude that the benefits of the Internet, particularly for females, outweigh the potential problems of communication and dating. We suggest you use the Internet to augment your spouse search. But remember: Be careful, ask questions, find out what you can about prospects before setting up dates and meet candidates in public places.

The number of men and women using computer dating sites is growing. An Internet search for "dating sites" will return results for many different types of services, including Match.com, eHarmony.com,

PlentyOfFish.com, Chemistry.com, PerfectMatch.com, Spark.com, SingleParentMeet.com, SeniorPeopleMeet.com, Matchmaker.com, ItsJustLunch.com and Date.com.

Additionally, many social networking sites are fertile sources of possible dating and spouse prospects. These include thousands of singles groups all over the United States and in other countries on sites such as Facebook and MySpace. Many of these social sites also show photos and often provide lots of personal information that you will find helpful.

The computer camera or webcam, if available, can be useful. Many newer machines have them built in. But even if you have an older computer or a new one without a camera, you can buy a webcam and add it to your computer. It will enable you to speak to and see another person, anywhere, at any hour, as long as both of you have webcams hooked up to your computers and as long as you are willing to see and be seen.

You can also use your computer to communicate by voice very inexpensively and efficiently. For example, the magicJack device allows you to use any computer as a telephone wherever you are (automobile, train, bus, etc.). Plug any telephone into your magicJack, then insert it into any USB port on your computer. Skype offers a similar online telephone and video conference service and there are more! An Internet search of "Voice Over Internet Protocol" (VOIP) can provide more information.

Today, any spouse seeker—even the most timid—can sit down at his or her computer (or relax in bed) at any hour, log on to one of the hundreds of dating Web sites and easily find many prospective single partners of similar age and with similar interests. Photos are usually displayed. Plus, the spouse seeker need not use his or her real name or any identifying information until he or she feels confident and ready to do so. The wonderful anonymity of the Internet empowers spouse seekers to shed their timidity and energetically search for Mr. or Ms. Right.

The point is that using the techniques we explain in this chapter, you can carry on your spouse hunt 24/7 from wherever you happen to be: at home, at work, on vacation, on a business trip, etc. VOIP and the ubiquitous personal computer have combined to make spouse hunting far less difficult now as compared to the past. The Internet, along with the evaluation method we explored in the first five chapters, provides an excellent method of simplifying the task of finding a potential spouse by allowing men and women to quickly "meet" and evaluate a large number of potential mates. Whereas traditional meeting and dating practices might require many months to meet and evaluate possible mates, the Internet can condense this into weeks (providing you utilize the Prospective Spouse Checklist, once you study and understand it).

Let's focus next on Janet, who learned about and used the checklist to find the right eligible man online.

Janet was a very attractive young woman who had just moved to Los Angeles for a new job. She was in the market for Mr. Right, but after two failed relationships in the years since she left college, she felt discouraged. Although the men she had been dating were eager to hop into bed (and some had been exciting), none seemed to have what she wanted: a combination of intelligence, warmth and compassion as well as interests that were compatible with hers. After Janet reviewed our Prospective Spouse Checklist and the explanations for each item, she decided on a new tactic. "I'm going to see who I might find on the Internet." She booted up her computer and logged onto one of the largest dating sites. She submitted her personal info as well as the age range of desired dates, plus some general criteria she desired: intelligence, height, weight, interests and hobbies. In short order, she had her pick of a large number of males in her new city. She started with Sam, a good-looking lawyer in his thirties who enjoyed reading, hiking and tennis.

She e-mailed him: "Sam, I saw your profile online. It sounds like we have similar interests. Tell me a little about yourself."

Just before she clicked *send* she thought to herself, *I just remembered that the first item on the checklist is single*, so she added to her e-mail, "Are you married or single?" Then she sent her message.

Surprisingly, within thirty minutes, she had a reply: "Janet—great to hear from you. I saw your picture and the other information you put online and it sounds like maybe we could meet for a drink. Pick a place and let's see what happens. What do you have to lose? I'm a partner in a large Los Angeles law firm. And, in answering your question, I am married, but I am in the process of getting a divorce. I'm eager to meet you."

As she read the end of the e-mail, Janet was shocked at first. *I'm stunned,* she thought. *This guy's write-up on the Web site looked great, but my first try turns up a guy who's married.* Janet smiled and said to herself, "Hey, look at the bright side. I avoided spending several hours digging for the truth, so I have time to try again!"

During the next two hours, she investigated eight candidates on the Web site and found two excellent prospects who e-mailed their telephone numbers to her. She did not give her number to them. She phoned and spoke to each of them. One of them had a webcam so they also video chatted for a few minutes and she liked what she saw. She arranged to meet each of them after work at a local restaurant.

Janet's example illustrates how you can enlarge your choice pool and save a great deal of time—perhaps weeks or even months—as long as you are careful. You can go through quite a few names during one evening in front of your computer. It is easy to avoid unwanted pursuers by taking some logical precautions: meet in public places and don't give identifying information until you are comfortable. Above all, remember: the larger your pool of possible spouse candidates, the more likely it is that you will find Mr. or Ms. Right in a shorter time!

Before making a date to meet, we suggest that during your first telephone discussion you cover some of the essential checklist points without being too pushy or obvious. It will save you time. For example, if you are single and want your own family, you may want to rule out someone who already has one or more children. If you have a college and post-graduate education, you may wish to confine your dating prospects to those who have at least college backgrounds. Generally, we suggest you talk fifteen to twenty minutes by telephone or webcam, having the checklist requirements in mind, and assure yourself that you are not wasting time and that he or she sounds attractive and worthwhile.

If you use the Internet the general objective is the same as if you happen to meet someone suggested by a friend: to locate someone who is promising and weed out those who do not merit further attention. You can also utilize technology with a relative or friend's introduction to be sure that the new prospective date really suits you. One woman who did this was Donna and the results were promising.

Donna received a call from Robert, who had obtained her number from Donna's cousin. When he called, Donna learned that Robert worked in law enforcement. She wondered, *Is he a policeman on the street or an agent? Does he carry a gun?* He sounded interesting so she asked him, "Do you have a webcam?"

"Sure do," Robert replied. "Shall we video chat online?" he suggested.

Donna liked this. She thought it showed that not only was he sensitive enough to see that she had some questions about him, but he also took the initiative in suggesting the video chat instead of requiring her to do so. Once they connected online she was impressed. He was nice looking and spoke well. They chatted for a few minutes and arranged to meet for a cocktail the following evening.

As soon as her call was over, Donna telephoned her cousin, who confirmed she had, in fact, given Donna's phone number to Robert. Through her cousin, Donna also obtained more information about him: he was about six feet tall, had a college degree and was thought to be up and coming in the local police department. He also enjoyed his role as first child from a family of four siblings. Donna appreciated her cousin's additional personal insights and was looking forward to meeting Robert.

Donna's example demonstrates the added advantage of a family or friend referral and also illustrates how a personal referral can take advantage of the Internet.

chapter seven

Overcoming the Challenges of Remarriage

The extremely high rate of divorce to which we've referred earlier has created a large population of men and women seeking compatible spouses for a second or even third time around. This pool of spouse seekers has been made even larger by the steady increase in lifespan throughout the world. The average United States male now lives beyond age seventy-two and his female counterpart will reach the age of eighty. When one spouse dies the survivor often reenters the marriage market.

However, second marriages are more complicated. Individuals often bring to the new relationship many of the same issues they brought to their first marriages. In addition, they are often left feeling disappointed, hurt and angry as a result of problems from the previous marriage. Widows or widowers may have experienced many loving and positive years with their spouses. Others' marriages may have been marred by stress and conflict that can affect any new relationships.

Some new unions will involve children. One or both partners may bring to the partnership children who range from infants to college age or older. Some may have adult children and grandchildren. Addressing their varied and individual needs complicates and adds stress to a new marriage. And younger couples may decide to add a child or children to this union. The successful blending of families is challenging.

After a failed marriage, most people are left with a legacy of conflicting emotions. They have lost their roles of being husbands or wives. Some feel they have been "demoted" to being "single again." They must reassess their identities as they begin the search for another relationship. Some view divorce as failure. Yet others feel they are "free" and feel relieved. Still others feel abandoned, deceived, enraged, suspicious or depressed.

For a combination of all of these reasons, those seeking a new spouse often come to the dating process burdened by intense emotions that may prevent or impede a fulfilling new relationship from developing. Those who are divorced or widowed find it difficult to reconnect. They may not have processed and faced the grief, anger and sadness that came from their losses.

FINANCIAL CONSIDERATIONS

When divorced people begin to date and court, they often mistakenly assume that they are financially free from previous obligations that originated during their first marriages. However, the newly divorced may still have joint ownership with the ex-spouse of a home, condominium or other assets. In addition, there may also be substantial liabilities of which they are unaware and which can seriously impact a new marriage. It is incumbent upon the couple to disclose and discuss such items with each other so there are no unpleasant surprises after the couple marries. Even though such discussions can be described as "unromantic," secrecy and silence are far worse and can easily destroy a marriage. On the other hand, if a serious problem like a large debt or the danger of serious illness is disclosed and discussed, the couple may still choose to marry and they will be far more able and willing to face and deal with such issues.

There are also important future financial considerations that require exploration. For example, will the new couple commingle their assets and income? Will both write checks on a joint bank account? If one or both of them have children, how will income be allocated between the old and new families? Also, as uncomfortable as the subject may be, the couple should discuss and consider what will happen to the assets if one of the partners dies. As they face and attempt the resolution of such issues openly, each partner has the opportunity to more accurately gauge the generosity, flexibility, judgment and other qualities of the prospective spouse. They will be able to gain valuable insight that will help both to feel comfortable about their marriage decision. Conversely, if intractable problems arise when these topics are discussed, each prospective partner has the right—and perhaps the obligation—to reevaluate their entire relationship and marriage decision.

We believe serious issues concerning a prior marriage should be pursued well before a couple decides to marry so that the couple will feel their new relationship is a committed one and they are comfortable enough to openly face and resolve such problems.

THE NEED FOR ADAPTABILITY

Those who have been single for many years, either because of divorce or a death, may have developed their own set of living routines. But they must be flexible enough to adjust to new and unfamiliar daily routines for a new relationship to take root.

One couple who had these issues was Jane and Jeffrey.

Jane, who was in her forties and had been single for more than ten years, had been dating Jeffrey, a fellow accountant in her firm, for about six months and felt they were falling in love. One evening at dinner he asked her if she would like to move in with him and his three children. Their mother had been killed in an automobile accident four years prior. Without much thought or discussion, Jane agreed. She was pleased to be asked and was glad to feel needed. She and Jeffrey seemed very compatible and she welcomed the opportunity to grow closer to Jeffrey and his family.

However, there was trouble from the very first week. Jeffrey expected her to participate in breakfast preparation, which eliminated her usual hour of quietly drinking coffee and reading the morning paper. Instead she was confronted with three demanding children needing clean clothes and school lunches as well as breakfast. Dinnertime was equally hectic. The children participated in after-school and late day sports activities. They needed to eat dinner early so that they could begin their homework. When she lived alone, Jane ate late—around eight o'clock—while enjoying her favorite television shows. But at Jeffrey's house, it seemed to her that the noise level remained constant and overwhelming. She could not understand the teenagers' music and constant disputes, conflicts and meltdowns over what she considered nothing.

For the first time in years she dreaded coming home from work. After four months Jane realized that she was not sufficiently flexible to adapt to Jeffrey's family. With some regret she told Jeffrey, "As much as I love you, it just won't work. I am too set in my ways to be comfortable participating in your active lifestyle." Jane moved back to her tranquil and well organized abode and eventually married a man with grown children.

The family issues in the Jane and Jeffrey relationship show that item 20: Flexible is an important item on the checklist to consider in remarriage, especially when children are involved.

REPEATING PRIOR MARRIAGE PROBLEMS
As divorced partners embark on the quest for spouses for new marriages, they must be careful not to repeat the mistakes that led to their failed first unions. They should take care that they are not, like Amanda in the next example, trading one problem for another.

Amanda divorced her husband, because he spent all their money on his cocaine habit, only to discover that her new prospect, Harry, had a serious drinking problem. She utilized our checklist and realized that his addiction was a red flag item. This helped her find the courage to end the relationship.

In another example, if sexual dysfunction was a primary cause of the divorce, it would be advisable to seek professional help prior to the second marriage. This is also true for any other major issue, particularly alcohol, drugs or gambling addictions, a partner's inability to control anger or other red flag items (discussed in chapter 3). If such problems had their roots in an early childhood experience, these matters can also be explored in therapy.

Remember the requirements for remarriage are basically the same as for a first marriage: a person who has the capacity to commit and sustain a relationship and who is a good match. The new spouse must also fulfill the four essential spouse roles of lover, friend, parent and business partner.

As partners resume dating, they should use the checklist just as Joan did during her dating period with Gary (chapter 4). It will provide a structure for them to evaluate potential spouses.

It is important that a divorced person gain some insight as to how he or she may have contributed to the breakup of the previous marriage as well as what behavior and issues the ex-spouse exhibited in their marriage that caused stress and conflict. Both partners often contribute to marital turmoil even though it may be to different degrees.

NO CHILDREN INVOLVED

Marrying for a second time when there are no children poses fewer complications and problems, because there are fewer persons with whom to interact and fewer individual needs to be considered.

However, as Flo in our next example found out, former spouses, living or dead, may still impact the relationship.

Flo met Lenny, a real estate agent, when she listed her and her ex-husband's condominium for sale. She had been divorced for several months and explained to Lenny that the court settlement provided for a prompt sale; she hoped Lenny would accomplish this. John, her ex-husband, was pressuring her, as he was anxious to split the proceeds.

"Well," said Lenny, "the market is not so great, so we'll have to price it for a quick sale."

To Flo's delight, Lenny called her two weeks later and told her he had a buyer. He suggested that they celebrate.

Flo said, "Okay, what would you like to do?"

Lenny replied, "How about dinner at eight? And I'll bring the papers for you to sign."

Dating began and Flo found out that Lenny was also divorced after a short marriage, which he described as "an unfortunate mistake." He explained to her that Kate, his ex-wife, was very focused on her law career, worked late every night from the start of the marriage and was obsessed with her cases. Also, he reported that she had refused to even consider having children. Kate wanted to become a partner in her law firm and felt that this would conflict with being a mother. "It was something we never discussed before we got married," explained Lenny.

All went well in Lenny and Flo's relationship, except Flo noticed Lenny had one irritating habit: Lenny often called her "Kate." Flo was hurt, despite Lenny's constant apologies. She wondered, *Deep down does he still care for her and is still in love with her?* But Flo didn't confront Lenny even though one night he called out Kate's name in his sleep. Nevertheless, over time, their relationship deepened and Flo began to feel that he was over his feelings for Kate and their first marriage seemed put to rest.

Lenny and Flo were both anxious to make a success of their forthcoming marriage, so they used the checklist to evaluate themselves and each other. They both scored well. Although they agreed they would have children, they had not yet discussed childcare, specifically whether or not Flo would be a stay-at-home mother or if she would promptly return to work after a baby arrived. Flo reread the explanation of the checklist item on agreement of major goals and childcare and told Lenny that she wanted to stay at home so she could parent their children.

Lenny told Flo frankly, "Look, I'd like to start our married life by building up our savings and investments and if you stay home as a housewife and mother and don't keep your job, it will be more difficult to save any money."

Flo disagreed and explained, "We are going to be married for many years. I can work after our children are in school, but while they are infants and preschoolers, I want to be there as their mother—not working."

At first Lenny was shocked. He had assumed that Flo was career-oriented and, like many mothers, would place the children in day care or have a nanny take care of them at home. But he could see how strongly she felt on this point. He also then recalled how much he had appreciated his own mother's presence when he was very young. He decided to defer to Flo's wishes and told her, "Flo, since you feel so strongly about this, give me two or three days to think about it. I guess we could handle this financially, but I don't want to be hasty, so I'd like to think about it just for a short while." Flo appreciated his response and was confident he would see it her way.

Flo and Lenny's story demonstrates how important it is for a couple to discuss major issues before marriage. These include having children and how finances and childcare will be handled. It also illustrates the important function of the checklist: it prompts couples to face and solve problems that might otherwise be forgotten and over-looked. Such problems can easily surface and cause conflict.

CHILDREN FROM PRIOR MARRIAGES

As difficult as a second marriage might be, it can be even more stress-ful if each parent brings children from earlier unions, a very common scenario for second marriages. Unlike first marriages, such couples face a formidable set of difficult problems:

- How will my new spouse parent my child?
- How will I parent my new stepchild?
- Will there be enough money for two families?
- Will this marriage bring up the same problems I faced in my first marriage?
- How will my ex-spouse relate to my new spouse?
- How will we handle holidays and celebrations?
- Will we be able to have a honeymoon and a real romance with the children around?
- What if my children don't like my new spouse and/or don't get along with their new stepsiblings?
- Do I know enough about this new spouse, especially his or her family history?
- Are we going to have children together?

After a remarriage, parents must face the many issues of step-parenting. Once the courtship, wedding and honeymoon are over, there may be a letdown in everyone's good behavior. A cheerful and loving bride or groom may morph into a "wicked stepmother" or "cruel stepfather." A previously amorous spouse may feel "too tired." A considerate and thoughtful husband may become demanding and insatiable. New stepsiblings, formerly cooperative, suddenly can begin to tease, fight and become oppositional. Money may be "hemorrhaging in all directions to people I don't even care about." The spouses may comment to each other, "How different this marriage is from our first marriages. We started those marriages with no children. We could play together as husband and wife. We didn't have so many obligations for school events, Little League games and recitals. Money wasn't designated for an ex-spouse. We were both biologically connected to our one new baby and we became bonded to our own child. We didn't worry about the marriage failing. We're now so much more conscious about having a lasting relationship."

There also may be significant benefits to remarriage involving children. Children may be pleased, because they feel they are now part of a stable family. An only child may enjoy having older or younger siblings. Children may feel protected and supported by two adult parents who are present (as compared to living with an unmarried parent who is busy working and dating).

As another positive, stepchildren can learn from the different talents, strengths and passions of the new stepparent. They can observe how their mother or father is able to relate in a positive and loving way to another partner in contrast to the conflict they saw in their parents' first marriage.

However, establishing a relationship with a stepchild is very different from forming a relationship with one's own child. Unless there has been a long period of getting acquainted stretching over many months, the new parent is abruptly thrust into the role of stepmother or stepfather. Children are catapulted into the role of stepchild as well, before an attachment has a chance to develop. Because this relationship has been quickly and artificially created, attachments and close feelings may be much more difficult to create, desirable though they may be. Visitation schedules can also disrupt the child's participation in the life of the new and blending family.

Some fathers feel they have failed with their own children and may give their stepchildren more time and affection. These issues sprang up in Henry and Jean's new marriage.

Henry, a hardworking salesman, was never home or available to his young wife and twins. The years passed, the marriage disintegrated and his values changed. When he married Jean he wanted to be a participating dad. He attended outings with his stepchildren and shared his interests and skills with them. His own children had been deprived of this kind of parenting while, over time, Jean's children developed a close bond with and affection for their stepfather.

DEALING WITH STEPCHILDREN

When children are involved, a couple contemplating a second marriage should discuss and reach agreement on some fundamental but quite complex questions:

- Where will the visiting stepchildren sleep? Will they have their own rooms? Will they have a separate place to keep their clothes and toys?
- How will we schedule the week and provide special time with each child and stepchild?
- How will we provide time to nurture our marriage?
- How will we celebrate holidays and birthdays? Will our ex-spouses be included in these events?
- How will the children's responsibilities be handled? Will the stepchildren have any chores or tasks when visiting?
- Will the biological parent or the stepparent make decisions about how the children are held accountable? What role will each parent play in discipline?
- Will the biological parent and stepparent back each other up in decisions concerning discipline and expectations? Often one of the parents will have a more realistic understanding of what is age-appropriate. Problems arise when either too much or too little is expected of the children.
- Do we plan to have our own biological child?

If the couple cannot discuss and agree on these matters, they need to ask themselves: Will our marriage work?

Hank and Cindy are a couple who realistically faced some of the issues of remarriage with children.

Hank and Cindy met one hot July afternoon at the neighborhood swimming club. They were both with their respective children who were enjoying the water. Hank's two sons, ages ten and twelve, were practicing their backstroke techniques, swimming laps and improving their diving skills. Cindy's young children were having fun in the shallow children's pool. Cindy sat in the shade under an overhang. Hank, sitting nearby, admired her great legs and beautiful tan.

Suddenly Hank saw a toddler go under the water. He leaped up and jumped into the pool, grabbing the child. Cindy, who had been temporarily distracted reading a magazine, looked up to see her daughter Bella coughing in Hank's arms. She bolted to his side in a state of panic and grabbed her now wailing daughter. Peter, her five-year-old who had left the pool, started to cry as well. Cindy was speechless.

Hank knelt and put his hand on Peter's shoulder. "Your sister will be fine. Let's all go and have a drink and some ice cream at the snack bar." Cindy thanked Hank but still felt overwhelmed by the events.

The following Sunday they met again at the pool. Cindy said gratefully, "All week long I've been thinking how your quick action saved Bella. Come for dinner with your two children next Friday night and we will celebrate the rescue."

Cindy had been divorced for over a year. Her husband had told her he felt "trapped" when Cindy unexpectedly became pregnant with their second child. He wanted "out."

Hank had been separated and then divorced after his wife had a series of mental breakdowns. Although they had joint custody, the children spent most of the time with him.

Hank and Cindy discovered they were very compatible and enjoyed being together with or without the children. Eventually, after months of dating, they discussed marriage. Many issues were explored dealing with the blending of the two families.

Hank explained that for practical purposes he was the primary caregiver for his children and was concerned about his ability to pay alimony, support his growing teenagers and assume the obligations of a new marriage. But he calculated that his income as an insurance executive along with the support received from Cindy's ex-husband would be sufficient to keep the family going. They planned that Cindy would be a stay-at-home parent, since for a significant part of the time she would be caring for all four children. In addition, they both agreed that they would require enough room in their home for Hank, Cindy and their respective children. Fortunately, Cindy had inherited her parents' home, which had three bedrooms. Currently each of her youngsters had his or her own room. They decided that after the marriage Cindy's young children would share a bedroom and Hank's boys would occupy the second bedroom. They would use the third. They also realized that some time in the future they might need more space as Cindy's son and daughter matured.

Hank was grateful that Cindy saw the need to provide privacy for his children. She even spoke about the need to consult them as to how they wanted to arrange the furniture and decorate the walls. She hoped that they would feel comfortable living with their new blended family.

Cindy also found herself to be anxious at the prospect of dealing with Hank's boys: their teenage moods, bathroom needs, TV watching and general adolescent behavior. After all, the house was small and they would naturally impact one another both positively and negatively. Before her first marriage, Cindy had been a junior high school English teacher and was well aware of the stresses early teenagers experienced. She understood that there were developmental differences between the early adolescent boys and her own younger children that needed to be addressed and respected.

Another issue concerned Cindy. While visiting, Hank's boys showed no interest in Peter and at times teased him, while they often indulged the cute two-year-old Bella. However, she felt that this issue could be dealt with at an appropriate time. Cindy thought, *I will try to treat them with respect and kindness. That goes for Hank as well.*

These partners demonstrate their abilities to communicate and face the many problems that will confront their newly blended family. They have few illusions, seem realistic and will be better prepared for the future stresses and conflicts that may arise. Under the most ideal circumstances it's not easy for six individuals to live together in one household without some issues developing. Hank and Cindy seem ready for the challenge!

It is important to prepare for difficult times and create realistic expectations for the future remarriage. In any family, it is unrealistic to expect to be a perfect mother or father or to expect children to behave appropriately at all times. When such expectations are not met, everyone involved experiences anger, disappointment and concern. Children from the most stable of homes sometimes test limits, have meltdowns or withdraw sullenly.

A mother who works, shops, cooks, cleans and launders to impress a new mate may, as time goes on, feel unappreciated. A father who is providing his hard-earned money for food, schooling and lessons for his stepchildren may not understand why they are antagonistic toward him. It will be helpful to anticipate such problems and candidly discuss them before embarking on a new marriage and a blending of the two families.

THE SECOND WEDDING

One factor to be considered when evaluating a new spouse is the person's empathy and flexibility in preparing for the new relationship. It is not enough to assume that "love will find a way." Ask reflective questions such as: How thoughtful is he or she in his or her approach to the many stresses and adjustments needed for our new blended family? Will he or she agree to discuss the issues involved? What part, if any, will the children play in the upcoming wedding ceremony? Who will supervise and care for them if and when we go on a honeymoon? The willingness of a potential spouse to acknowledge these issues and discuss possible solutions is a very positive sign for the success of the marriage. However, if the future spouse is reluctant to face these issues, it is a warning sign indicating trouble ahead for the relationship.

Pamela and Arthur were seeing a number of warning signs.

Pamela found that she was becoming more and more distressed about Arthur's inability to consider their four children in relation to their forthcoming marriage and honeymoon. He had been creative and enthusiastic about their wedding. The guest list included a large number of his business associates and he had taken a leading role in planning the wedding entertainment. He had also spent considerable effort in planning their extensive honeymoon in the Bahamas. But he refused to discuss how his children and stepchildren could be included as participants in the upcoming festivities. Nor would he discuss who would care for the children during their ten-day honeymoon.

Pamela found herself increasingly distressed by his lack of interest in her two daughters. She also began to notice that he seldom even mentioned his own two children. Pamela thought, *I realize the wedding has been planned and is only two months away, yet only last night, after one of his business dinners, I felt distressed when he actually told me, "I don't even want to think about the children—mine or yours. Isn't it enough that I work hard and foot the bill for our wedding and honeymoon? Give me a break!"*

Pamela realized that she had been too hasty in accepting his marriage proposal, which occurred after only a few months of being wined and dined. She also realized that she had not had the opportunity to observe Arthur in a family environment. He had never stayed overnight with her and her two children. Nor had she spent any significant time with his children. It had been agreed that his two children would be spending half the time with him and half the time with his ex-wife. Since Pamela had full custody of her own two children, that meant all six of them would be spending a large amount of time together. She had fantasized, up to that point, that her future spouse would act as an involved father for her children, replacing, in a sense, their own dead father. She also found that she had been having many sleepless nights. Pamela now realized that she had been in a state of denial and had not faced the fact that was becoming increasingly clear: Her marriage would fail, because she needed an active, involved parent for both her children and his children. She thought to herself, *Arthur isn't the right person for me and the children. I'm glad that we haven't yet mailed out the wedding invitations.*

Difficult though it may have been for her, Pamela showed good judgment in ending her engagement and calling off the wedding. She showed much courage in making this decision. This example illustrates how important it is for a couple to consider all members of the new blended family. It also sheds light on the many new factors that couples must take into account the second time around when children's needs and feelings must be carefully considered. Had Pamela and Arthur utilized the checklist and arranged more family time together, Arthur's negative approach to parenting would have been more obvious and the relationship would have terminated long before wedding arrangements were made.

REMARRIAGE AFTER THE DEATH OF A SPOUSE
Eventually, the intense grief experienced from the death of a spouse will wane and the time widows and widowers consider remarriage

will arrive. But they face many additional issues that do not arise in a divorce. For example, if their marriage with the deceased was loving and fulfilling, many widows and widowers may feel disloyal and unfaithful to the memory of the departed husband or wife. Some terminally ill spouses, before death, actually give permission and verbalize their desires that spouses go on with their lives and seek happiness with others. But others communicate a much different message: Beware of the woman or man who will take advantage of you and your assets.

Those who have experienced good marriages have exhibited the capacity to sustain relationships. It has been shown clinically that a good first marriage creates the foundation for a satisfying second marriage. But it also true that some marriages may have been bitter, painful and disappointing. Those who were so involved require careful evaluation because of this question: What part did the survivor play in his or her disappointing previous marriage?

It is also important, from the standpoint of spouse selection, that the bereaved has allowed sufficient time to recover from the loss. If this has not occurred and if there is a premature effort to reenter the dating scene, there may be a serious inability on the part of the bereaved (as well as the new intended spouse) to genuinely commit, as well as an inability to properly fulfill the four essential spouse roles.

If grief is not resolved, the bereaved spouse prospect may be depressed, anxious and preoccupied. Six months or a year may be required before emotional equilibrium can be reestablished.

If the widow or widower has children, this further complicates the issue of remarriage. The children have experienced the profound loss of their parent and must also go through the mourning process. They require understanding, empathy and a stepparent as well as a parent who are responsive to their disappointments, angers and worries. After the parental death the child may view the potential spouse as an intruder, feeling as though he or she may deprive the child of time and affection from the surviving biological parent. Young children may feel a sense of needed protection and added security that is supplied by a new stepparent, but it may take considerable time for an attachment to develop between young children and a new stepparent.

In addition, if the deceased left adult children, whether or not living in the house, they may respond negatively to the idea of a parent who chooses to remarry. There also may be economic factors that cause problems. For example, children may be anxious about losing their expected inheritance, which they fear will be co-opted by a new stepparent. But other adult children may feel a sense of relief that someone will now nurture and care for the widowed parent.

Prenuptial financial agreements may also be considered, particularly if the couple is older, had been married for many years previously and acquired considerable assets before the death occurred. This agreement will usually focus on what can occur, whether the second marriage ends in divorce or death or even if it continues for a number of years. It may also provide for the separation of assets or what monies may be commingled for living expenses, travel and entertainment. For example, the prenuptial agreement may specifically provide that a portion or all of the assets be disposed of in such a way that they are placed completely outside the reach of the new spouse. Or there may be other specific property dispositions that will have other impacts.

The prospective husband and wife should carefully discuss and consider all provisions of any prenuptial agreement. Lawyers for one or both may also participate and suggest provisions that may confuse the couple involved. This can provoke controversy since a lawyer's obligation is strictly to his or her client (the future husband or wife). Consequently, many proposed marriages are derailed due to overzealous or insensitive attorneys. Therefore, great care must be taken by both prospective partners when dealing with prenuptial agreements.

There could also be anxiety about sexual activity and intimacy, particularly with older widows and widowers. They may have the additional problem of having to come to grips with their sexual memories involving the deceased spouse.

Ken and Amy, a middle-aged widow and widower, are a couple whose second marriage brought up a number of important issues to consider.

Ken and Amy met in a bereavement group for spouses. Amy had been happily married for over twenty years. Her husband died from a heart attack at age fifty-two while jogging early one morning in the park. The shock was profound. After six months of grieving and disbelief, Amy was persuaded by her friends to join a support group.

Ken, age fifty-five, had been married to his high school sweetheart who died of breast cancer after a painful three-year illness. Even though her death was anticipated, he felt lost, abandoned and lonely. His own parents had died years ago. His children were finishing their educations and dealing with their own issues. He was depressed and thought, *I have no one to care for and no one to really care for me.* A coworker suggested that many of his patients who had lost a spouse had been helped by a particular therapist who ran a local bereavement support group. Ken joined with some trepidation.

In the group, Ken and Amy sat across from each other. Ken responded to the way Amy described her marriage. He admired the life Amy and her husband had lived together and the adventures and many interests they had shared. Amy, after learning Ken's history, was impressed with Ken's commitment and devotion as well as his ability to nurture his ailing wife.

After the fourth session Ken asked Amy to join him for coffee. Dinner and a movie came next. In the weeks that followed both found that they enjoyed each other's company. They both needed a friend. Fortunately, their children were on their own and both had comfortable incomes. Although each was still mourning the loss of his or her respective spouse, they began developing a warm relationship.

Homebound for the last three years, Ken was ready to participate in more stimulating and varied activities. With Amy's company, travel now seemed a pleasant possibility. Amy also appreciated Ken's support and looked forward to his providing a safe and predictable presence.

Though they had begun feeling comfortable and were attracted to each other, both Ken and Amy felt anxious about participating in their first sexual intimacy, with each worrying about their abilities to recreate the excitement and pleasure they experienced in their previous marriages. Amy was concerned that age and gravity had had its effect on her body. At fifty she was not the firm and fit twenty-one-year-old of her youth. In spite of their apprehension, both of them were pleasantly surprised at experiencing mutual erotic pleasure during a weekend at a country resort.

During the bereavement sessions, Amy and Ken had learned about each other's marriage and early family stresses. As a result they had a head start in gaining insight and understanding about each other's issues and concerns. The group itself was an experience they both shared. It provided a basis of much conversation and humor as they reminisced about the group.

After a year of dating, they made the decision to move in together as prelude to a second marriage.

Ken and Amy were fortunate to be able to anticipate a second marriage that will provide companionship, support and affection after each experienced the loss of his or her first spouse.

REMARRIAGE: USING THE CHECKLIST

Every couple contemplating remarriage hopes that it will be success-ful and fulfilling. This is true regardless of the way the previous union ended, whether by death or divorce. If one or both of the first mar-riages were unhappy, each partner will wish to avoid the pitfalls and circumstances that put stress on the first marriages and contributed to their failures. The partners should be able to understand the stresses of living together as well as what can sabotage a relationship. They also need to be aware of mistakes they made, which should help them to avoid repeating these behaviors. Prospective spouses should reflect on their first marriages:

- Was my first marriage happy or unhappy? Were we a good match? Did we both have the capacity to commit?
- What were the personality factors or events which doomed the marriage?
- What factors and qualities of my early childhood relationships influenced my marriage?

We suggest the simple method of using the checklist to answer these questions and to increase the odds of achieving a successful remarriage. Compare the "YES" and "NO" responses that would have applied to your prior spouse with those for your prospective partner. Be aware that if you find the answers for your former and prospective spouse are similar you may be recreating the same neg-ative script. Using the checklist may also help reveal what actually caused the earlier relationship to fail. Most important, it can serve as a warning to think carefully and to take the time needed to make an informed decision about the prospective marriage.

Conclusion

We appreciate the real difficulties involved in finding the right spouse. Luck and chance will play their parts, but none of us can count on luck. It will require courage, ingenuity and persistence, but the goal is well worth the effort.

The real challenge is to locate, evaluate and exchange vows with a partner who has the capacity to sustain and commit to a relationship and who can also be a compatible partner. Locating a spouse who will fulfill the four essential marital roles (friend, parent, business partner and lover) is no easy task. Difficult though it may be, it is probably life's most important and rewarding endeavor.

Human beings thrive on attachments. Survival depends on those caring individuals from the moment we are born and enter the world until old age, when again we need nurturing and care. For most of us a companion, friend or relative in close proximity creates a feeling of security and well-being. Finding a committed loving partner at almost any stage in life is valuable whether we formally marry or not.

Our age and normal developmental changes may influence our expectations as we evaluate potential mates. What we value in a partner often changes as we leave our twenties, thirties and forties and enter our fifties and sixties. Sexual compatibility is often of paramount importance to a young couple, but an older spouse seeker may look for a partner who can provide a secure lifestyle and companionship. Women in their late thirties may be concerned that their childbearing years may be passing. They may want to find a partner who will help create a child and function as a competent and nurturing parent.

As one grows older, the pool of eligible and available men and women becomes smaller. The decision to marry is often influenced by the fear of being single and alone and the need to form a secure attachment. A person may feel pressure to marry and may settle for someone who might be a marital risk and score poorly on the Prospective Spouse Checklist. Some people at this stage may marry realizing there is a tradeoff and enter into their marriages aware of and prepared for some of the conflicts and pitfalls ahead.

We have an abiding need for relationships to provide affection, stimulation, protection and security. Hopefully marriage will be a long, interesting and fun journey, with some problems that you will be well equipped to overcome. True love need not be relegated to books, movies or television dramas. Many of us can achieve this ideal by exploring the issues that we have been discussing during courtship and before marriage.

The Authors' Journey

When we met, Dr. Isabelle Fox was a junior at Radcliffe. Co-author Robert M. Fox, a United States Navy Ensign and recent graduate of the University of Pennsylvania's Wharton School, was in the process of leaving his aircraft carrier and preparing for discharge into civilian life. Robert's cousin, who was a classmate of Isabelle's, arranged the introduction.

On our first date we went for a drink and within the first half hour we discussed the book *Ideal Marriage* by the Dutch gynecologist Theo H. Van de Velde. Although it was first published in 1926, this book is still very readable and its sexual instruction is as timely today as it was then.[1] It certainly was a unique and unusual subject to explore within the first few minutes after meeting. Dating and courtship continued for over a year and we now realize that during that time we considered many of the essential concepts now contained in our Prospective Spouse Checklist. Over our many years of marriage (the first and only for both of us) we have experienced the four roles discussed in our book: lover, friend, parent and business partner. Using our experience, we have attempted to present spouse seekers with an organized and systematic approach for selecting and evaluating potential mates.

We are delighted that, with luck playing its part, our marriage has lasted so successfully. While we agree that our happiness and our personal history will not necessarily be replicated by all who read our book, we do suggest that our rational approach will help readers as they consider the most significant decision of their lives: Whom to marry?

In the end, we hope that our readers will achieve the same objective that we envisioned when we met: to find a compatible spouse who will join in a lifetime of love, affection, stimulation, support, shared adventures and challenges, so that they too may "live happily ever after."

WHAT WE NEED FROM OUR SPOUSES
By Isabelle Fox

We need the warmth of a snuggle and a caress
We need to hear words of affection and encouragement
We need to feel protected and safe
We need to share worries, disappointments and angers
We need to trust
We need occasionally to be fed, pampered and indulged
We need erotic pleasure as our bodies merge
We need the stimulation of ideas and goals
We need to share in the joys and tribulations of parenthood
We need to join in laughter, celebrations and tears
We need support in times of stress, separation and loss
And in the end we need to be loved, cherished and nurtured
By someone who is "there"

Acknowledgements

We are truly grateful for the support and encouragement from our immediate family: Michael, James and Carolyn, their spouses and children. Over the years the concept of the checklist has evoked both interest and humor as this book was conceived and in progress.

We are deeply indebted to The Bowlby Attachment Study group: Drs. Diana Taylor, Robin Davis, Nick Stefanidis, Mary Duchette, Pat Sable, Lisa Margolis and Louise Billman for their continuing insights and help in validating the attachment concepts in the text. Most of us studied with and were inspired by Dr. John Bowlby, the father of attachment theory.

In addition, our friends Christina and Bill Davidson, Sheila Segal, Hermine and Arthur Kovacs, Barbara Nicholson, Liza Parker and Paulita Neal have been supportive of this project and have generously shared their wisdom with us. Appreciation is extended to Adrienne Berman, Vicki Siegel and Susann Bauman, who have patiently listened to our trials and tribulations as the book came to fruition.

We offer many thanks for the undying efforts of our agent, Nancy Rosenfeld. Much gratitude is also extended to Cheri Singer for her tireless work on the manuscript.

Lastly we need to congratulate each other on the fact that our marriage has survived the many minor yet intense arguments as we co-authored this book. Our love and affection has endured.

Notes

Preface

[1] David McCullough, *John Adams* (New York: Simon and Schuster, 2001).

[2] Annie Casey Foundation, Baltimore, MD, National Kids Count Program, http://blank.kidscount.org, 2007/2008.

[3] Joyce A. Martin, et.al., "Births: Final Data for 2008," US Department of Health and Human Services, 59, no 1, December 2010, http://www.cdc.gov/nchs/data/nvsr/nvsr59/nvsr59_01.pdf.

[4] John Gottman and Nan Silver, *The Seven Principles for Making Marriage Work* (New York: Three Rivers Press, 1999).

[5] Harold H. Kelley, et. al., *Close Relationships* (New York: W.H. Freeman, 1983).

[6] Daniel Goleman, *Emotional Intelligence* (New York: Bantam Books, 1995).

[7] Erich Fromm, *The Art of Loving* (New York: Bantam Books, 1956).

Chapter One

[1] Nathaniel Branden, "A Vision of Romantic Love," in *The Psychology of Love*, ed. Robert J. Sternberg and Michael L. Barnes (New Haven: Yale University Press, 1988).

2   Bernard Murstein, "A Taxonomy of Love" in *The Psychology of Love*, ed. Robert J. Sternberg and Michael L. Barnes (New Haven: Yale University Press, 1988).

3   Stanton Peele and A. Brodsky, *Love and Addiction* (New York: NAL, 1976).

4   Murstein, "A Taxonomy of Love."

5   Phillip Shaver, Cindy Hazen and Donna Bradshaw, "Love as Attachment: The Integration of Three Behavioral Systems" in *The Psychology of Love*, ed. Robert J. Sternberg and Michael L. Barnes (New Haven: Yale University Press, 1988).

6   George Levinger, "Can We Picture 'Love'?" in *The Psychology of Love*, ed. Robert J. Sternberg and Michael L. Barnes (New Haven: Yale University Press, 1988).

7   Richard von Krafft-Ebing, *Psychopathia Sexualis* (New York: Pioneer Publications, 1945).

8   Havelock Ellis, *Studies in the Psychology of Sex* (Philadelphia, PA: F.A. Davis, 1928).

9   David Goicoechea, ed., *The Nature and Pursuit of Love: The Philosophy of Irving Singer* (Amherst, NY: Prometheus Books, 1995), 183-185.

10 Albert Ellis, *The American Sexual Tragedy* (New York: Twayne, 1954).

11 Pamela Regan, "Romantic Love and Sexual Desire," in *Romantic Love and Sexual Behavior: Perspectives from the Social Sciences*, ed. Victor C. De Munck (Westport, CT: Praeger Publishers, 1998).

12 Ellen Berscheid, "Whatever Happened to Old-Fashioned Lust?" in *The Psychology of Love*, ed. Robert J. Sternberg and Michael L. Barnes (New Haven: Yale University Press, 1988).

13 John Alan Lee, "Love-Styles," in *The Psychology of Love*, ed. Robert J. Sternberg and Michael L. Barnes (New Haven: Yale University Press, 1988).

14 Branden, "A Vision of Romantic Love".

15 Dean Ornish, *Love and Survival* (New York: Harper Collins, 1998).

16 David Buss, *The Evolution of Desire* (New York: Basic Books, 1994).

17 Nuna Alberts, "The Science of Love (the Chemistry of Romance)," *Life* (February 1999) 46.

18 Buss, *The Evolution of Desire.*

19 Alice H. Eagly, *Sex Differences in Social Behavior: A Social Role Interpretation* (Hillsdale, NJ: Lawrence Erlbaum Associates, Inc., Publishers, 1987).

20 David C. Geary, *Male, Female: The Evolution of Human Sex Differences* (Washington, DC: American Psychological Association, 1998).

21 Deborah Blum, *Sex on the Brain* (New York: Penguin Books, 1997).

22 Ibid.

Chapter Three

1   Caitlin Flanagan, "Is There Hope for the American Marriage?" *Time*, July 2, 2009, http://www.time.com/time/nation/article/0,8599,1908243,00.html.

2   John Bowlby, *The Making and Breaking of Affectional Bonds* (London: Tavistock Publications, 1979).

3   Isabelle Fox, *Being There: The Benefits of a Stay-at-Home Parent* (New York: Barron's, 1996).

4   Shaver, Hazen and Bradshaw, "Love as Attachment: The Integration of Three Behavioral Systems."

5   Fox, *Being There.*

6   Ibid.

7   Judith Wallerstein and Sandra Blakeslee, *The Good Marriage* (New York: Warner Books, 1995).

8   Walter Toman, *Family Constellation: Its Effect on Personality and Social Behavior* (New York: Springer Publishing, 1993) and William Cane, *The Birth Order Book of Love: How the #1 Personality Predictor Can Help You Find "the One"* (Cambridge, MA: De Capo Press, 2008).

9   Marsha Lee Hudgens, *Good People, Bad Marriages: Wisdom to Know, Freedom to Choose, Courage to Change* (Dickson, TN: Estuary Publishing, 1996).

10 Kalman Heller, "Improving the Odds for Successful Second Marriages," Parenting and Marital Advice, http://www.drheller.com/2ndmarriages.html.

11 David Biella, "What is the best age difference for husband and wife?" *Scientific American,* December 5, 2007.

12 Buss, *The Evolution of Desire* and Jeffry Larson, *Should We Stay Together?* (San Francisco: Jossey-Bass, 2000).

13 Buss, *The Evolution of Desire.*

14 Susan Saulny, "Black? White? Asian? More Young Americans Choose All of the Above," *New York Times,* January 30, 2011.

15 Jenifer L. Bratter and Rosalind B. King, "'But Will It Last?': Marital Instability Among Interracial and Same-Race Couples," *Family Relations* 57 (April 2008).

16 Donn Byrne and Sarah Murnen, "Maintaining Loving Relationships" in *The Psychology of Love,* ed. Robert J. Sternberg and Michael L. Barnes (New Haven: Yale University Press, 1988).

17 Buss, *The Evolution of Desire.*

18 Gottman and Silver, *The Seven Principles for Making Marriage Work.*

19 Bowlby, *The Making and Breaking of Affectional Bonds.*

20 Ken Magid and Carole McKelvey, *High Risk: Children without a Conscience* (New York: Bantam, 1989).

21 Wallerstein and Blakeslee, *The Good Marriage.*

22 Fox, *Being There.*

23 Karen Walant, *Creating the Capacity for Attachment: Treating Addictions and the Alienated Self* (Lanham, MD: Jason Aronson, 1999).

24 Penelope Leach, *Children First: What Society Must Do—and is Not Doing—for Children Today* (New York: Vintage, 1995).

25 Flanagan, "Is There Hope for the American Marriage?"

26 Larson, *Should We Stay Together?*.

27 Ibid.

28 Mark Goulston, *The 6 Secrets of a Lasting Relationship* (New York: Perigee Trade, 2002).

29 Buss, *The Evolution of Desire.*

30 Goulston, *The 6 Secrets to a Lasting Relationship.*

31 Fox, *Being There.*

32 Larson, *Should We Stay Together?*.

33 Bowlby, *The Making and Breaking of Affectional Bonds.*

34 Buss, *The Evolution of Desire.*

35 Charles T. Hill, Zick Rubin and Letitia Anne Peplau, "Breakups Before Marriage: The End of 103 Affairs," *Journal of Social Issues* 32 (1976), 147-168.

36 Berscheid, "Whatever Happened to Old-Fashioned Lust?"

37 Philip Blumstein and Pepper Schwartz, *American Couples* (New York: Simon and Schuster, 1983).

38 Wendy Williams and Michael Barnes, "Love Within Life," in *The Psychology of Love*, ed. Robert J. Sternberg and Michael L. Barnes (New Haven: Yale University Press, 1988).

39 Robert Frank, *The Involved Father* (New York: St. Martin's Press, 1999).

40 Blumstein and Schwartz, *American Couples.*

41 Ibid.

42 "How to Deal with Your Family if They Do Not Accept Your Date," Mama's Health, http://www.mamashealth.com/dating/biracial/default.asp.

[43] Janet Woitiz, *Marriage on the Rocks* (Deerfield Beach, FL: Health Communications, Inc, 1979).

Chapter Five

[1] Colin M. Parkes and J. Stevenson-Hinde, eds, *The Place of Attachment in Human Behavior* (New York: Basic Books, 1982).

[2] John Bowlby, *Loss: Sadness and Depression*, vol. 3 of *Attachment and Loss* (New York: Basic Books, 1980).

[3] Larson, *Should We Stay Together?*.

[4] Ibid.

[5] Flanagan, "Is There Hope for the American Marriage?"

Chapter 6

[1] Joy Browne, *Dating for Dummies* (Foster City, CA: IDG Books, 1997).

[2] Robert M. Fox, "Guess Who's Coming to Graduate School?" unpublished.

Afterword

[1] Theodore H. Van de Velde, *Ideal Marriage: Its Physiology and Technique* (New York: Random House, 1957).

index

abandonment, 65, 69, 76, 150, 182

abuse, 37, 39, 64, **65**, 67, 71, 76, 78, 84, 96, 98, 149; normative, 67

adaptability, 183

addiction/addictive behavior, 19, **24**, 40, 47, 71, 78, **117**–21, 141–2, 146–7, 151, 185

adolescents, 66, 192

adulthood, young, 37

advice, **24**–27, 81, 98–100

affection, 2, 11, 28, 34, 65, 77, 81–82, 103, 105, 114–115, 142, 157, 189–90, 196–197, 202, 204

age difference, **23**, 39, **48**–49

Alberts, Nuna, 6, 209

alcohol, 15, 17, 19–20, **24**, 35, 39–40, 71, 78, 96, 98, **117**–18,120–21, 131–2, 137–46, 151, 185

anger control, **24**, 39–40, **96**–98, 124–25, 141, 185

anxiety, 78–80, 98, 106, 149, 198

assets, **23**, **61**–2, **111**, 121, 173, 182–83, 196–97

attachment, 3, 27–28, 33, 35–36, 39, 64–65, 67, 69, 75–76, 79–80, 82, 86, 115, 117, 149–151, 189, 197, 201–2

Barnes, Michael, 106, 211

bereavement, 198–99

Berscheid, Ellen, 3, 208

Biella, David, 48, 210

birth order, 38–39

Blakeslee, Sandra, 36, 209

Blum, Deborah, 9, 209

Blumstein, Philip, 103, 109, 112, 211

boredom, 102–103

Bowlby, John, 29, 65, 98, 150, 209, 210, 211, 212

Bradshaw, Donna, 2, 34, 208, 209

Branden, Nathaniel, 1, 3, 207, 208

Bratter, Jenifer L., 54, 210

Brodsky, A., 1, 208

Browne, Joy, 168, 212

business partner, **22**, 31–32, 111, 185

Buss, David, 5, 7, 8, 51, 62, 82, 100, 209, 210, 211

Byrne, Donn, 55, 210

camera, web and computer, 175, 177–8

Cane, William, 38, 210

caregiver, 33–35, 62, 67–69, 75, 109, 122, 151; roulette, 35, 67, 69, 71

cheating, 48, 106, 108

cheerful, **23**, 81, **84**–85, 156

child support, 44–45, 161

child visitation, 43–45, 161, 189

childhood, 33–37, 65–66, 71, 74, 76, 78–80, 85–86, 98

commitment, capacity to form, 9, **22**, 33–37, 41, 70, 86

companionship, 5–7, 49, 102, 149, 202

computer, 124, 166, 169, 174–7

conflict, **24**, 30–32, 39, 44, 55, 61, 70, 73, 78, 84, 91–96, 99–100, **105**–123, 152–3, 181–9, 193

considerate, **23**, 27, **81**–83, 99

culture, 7–8, **23**, 54–55, 61, 166

custody, 43, 161, 190

death: of child, 7, 46, 66–67; of parent, 66, 78, 123, 196–7; of spouse, 183, 195–8, 200

depression, 78–79, 81, 83–86, 115, 122, 150, 155–6, 182, 196, 198

discipline, 30, 98, 190

divorce, 3, 12, 19, 29, 40, 42–45, 47–48, 54, 66, 70–73, 76, 78, 94, 96, 120, 131, 141, 160–1, 181–6, 196–7, 200

drinking. See alcohol

drugs, **23**, **24**, 35, 40, 78, 96, **117**–18, 120, 185

Eagly, Alice, 8, 209

educational difference, **23**, 39, **51**–52, 54, 83, 178

Ellis, Albert, 2, 208

Ellis, Havelock, 2, 11, 208

emotional factors, 3–4, 9, 11, 22, **23–24**, 48, 65–66, 68–70, 74, 78, 80, 85–86, 98, 117, 122, 149–51, 160–1, 182, 196

empathy, 104, 114, 193,196

engagement, 26–27, 30, 40, 70, 79, 91, 111, 117, 124–5, 145–7, **149**, 152, 154, 159–60

enjoy time together, **24**–27, 40, 52–53, 84, **102**–3, 147, 159

erotic passion, 3, 9, 29, 39, 204

ethical issues, **24**, 40, **105**–6, 123

family: blended, 45, 188–195; extended, 115; history, **23**, 29–30, 36, 41, **64**–80, 129–132, 188

female, what she wants, 5, **8**–11

finances, 31–32, 111–113, 187

Flanagan, Caitlin, 29, 70, 160, 209, 211, 212

flexible, **24**, 38, **90**–92, 99, 109, 158–9, 183–4

Fox, Isabelle, 34, 35, 67, 84, 203, 204, 209, 210, 211

Fox, Robert M., 172, 203, 212

Frank, Robert, 109, 211

Freud, Sigmund, 2, 11

friend, 4, 11, 20, 21, **23**, **25**–27, 71, 75, **86**–87, 105, 157, 167–8, 170, 178–9, 185, 201

friendship, 2, 7, 12, **86**

Fromm, Erich, xi, 207

gambling, 19–20, **24**, 31, 40, 106, **117**–118, **121**, 151, 185

Geary, David C., 8, 209

generous, 9, **24**, 31, 81, **100**–101, 104, 183

Goicoechea, David, 2, 208

Goleman, Daniel, xi, 207

Gottman, John, x, 62, 207, 210

Goulston, Mark, 81, 83, 211

graduate school, 52, 172–3

grandparents, **23**, 37, 40, 71, **74**–76, 142, 167

groups, social, educational and others, 55–56, 159–160, **169**–175, 198–9

Hazen, Cindy, 2, 34, 208, 209

health, emotional/physical/mental, 3, 10, **23**–**24**, 41, 49, 65, **78**–79, 111, 118–19, **122**–3

Heller, Kalman, 48, 210

Hill, Charles T., 102, 211

Hudgens, Marsha Lee, 40, 210

humor, sense of, **23**, 25, **83**–84, 91

illness, major, **23**, **24**, 66–67, 78–80, 120, **122**–123, 198

income, 9, **23**, 31, **61**–64, 100, 109, 111–12, 114, 121, 173, 183

infant, 2, 7, **23**, 34–35, 45, **67**–69, 71, 84, 181, 187; mortality, 7

intellectual factors, 4, 9, **23**, 51–53, 170

intelligence, 2, 9, 10, **23**, **51**–54, 172–174

interests: differing, 26, 53, 72, 91; similar, 29, 102, 165–6, 173, 175–6

Internet, 163, 167, 169, **174**–9

judgment, 4, **23**, 31, 48, 62, 81, **88**–90, 99, 111, 116, 132–3, 140–1, 149

Kelley, Harold H., x, 207

kind, **23**, 27, **81**–83, 99

King, Rosalind B., 54, 210

Krafft-Ebing, R. von, 2, 208

Larson, Jeffry H., 51, 74, 77, 78, 90, 153, 159, 210, 211, 212

Leach, Penelope, 68, 211

Lee, John Alan, 3, 208

legal problems, **24**, 39, **123**–4

Levinger, George, 2, 208

listening, 25, 27, 38, 99

living together, 90–91, 94, **153–**
161

loss, 65–66, 96, 150–1, 182,
196, 199

love, definition, 1–3

lover, 2, 20, 21, **27–29**, 157,
185, 201

lust, 2, 24, **103**. *See also* sexual
desire

Magid, Ken, 65, 210

male-female differences, **5–11**

male, what he wants, **5–8**

marital satisfaction, 51, 81

marriage, previous, **23**, 30, 47–
48, **181–2**, 185, 196, 199–200

marriage requirements, 6, **11–**
12, 22, 25–41, 54, 105, 157,
178, 185

marriage, second, 44–48, 181,
185, 188, 190, 196–199; remarriage, **181–200**

Martin, Joyce A., x, 207

match, 22, **24**–25, 30, 32, **37–**
41, 47, 52, 54, **115**-16, 146,
154, 169, 185, 200

matchmakers, **169**

McCullough, David, ix, 207

McKelvey, Carole, 65, 210

messiness, 94–96

money management, **24**, 31–32,
62, 90, 100–102, 106–7, **111–**
14, 154–5, 185, 187–9

mood, 85–86, 156

morality, 5, **24**, 40, **105**–108,
123

Murnen, Sarah, 55, 210

Murstein, Bernard, 1, 208

mutuality, 2, 11, **24–29**, 41, 54,
99, **102**–105, 114, 128, 149,
157, 159–60

neatness, **24**, 31, **93**–96

neglect, 35, 37, **65**, 76, 78–79,
84, 120

nuclear family, 29, 70, 100

nurturing, 28, 34, 81, 100, 122,
153, 157–8, 190, 197, 201,
204; checklist, **157**–8; in early
years, **23**, 29–30, 33–35, 37,
40, **65**–66, 74–75, 78, 98,
119–20

optimism, 34, 84

organized, **24**, 31, 81, **93**–96

Ornish, Dean, 3, 209

parent, as spousal role, 20–21,
29–30, 86, 101; death of, 66,
78, 123, 196–7

parents, abuse by, 64, 76–77,
97–98, 149; acceptance of
match by, **24**, 56, 60, **115**–16;
affection between, **23**, 77–78;
divorce of, **23**, **70**–72, 76,
129–32, 141–2; health of, **23**,
78–80, 85, 118–20, 132; relationship with, **23**, 40, 66, **70**–
72, **74**–78, 131

Parkes, Colin, 150, 212

Peele, Stanton, 1, 208

penny pinching 100–101

Peplau, Letitia Anne, 102, 211

personality traits, 9, 20, **23–24**, 31, 38, 41, **81**–102, 200

pets, **24**, 82, **114**–115

political views, **24**, 40, 90, **105**–106

pool of prospects, 10, 150, **164**–8, 171, 174, 177, 180, 202

pregnancy, 7, 9–10, 30, 104, **160**

problem areas, 19–20, **23–24**, 40–41, 47, 57, 61, 70, 74–75, 78–80, **117**–25, 146, 160, 182, **184–189**, 197–8

professional help, 37, 80, 83, 94, 104, 185

prompt, **24**, **92**–93

proximity: of children's parents, 2, 34; of partners, 102, 149, 201

punishment, 35, 98

race, **23**, **54**–55, 61

rape, 76

Regan, Pamela, 3, 208

rejection, 76, 105, 117, 150–1

religion, **23**, **24**, 40, **54**–61, 90–91, **108**–111, 116, 154, 166

relatives, 36, 76, **167**–8, 201

rigid, **24**, **90**–91, 109

roles of the spouse, 8, 20, **21**–22, 25–33, 41, 54, 78, 102, 104, 111, 122, 154, 157, 182, 185, 189–90, 196, 201

romantic love, 1–9, 64, 103, 207–8

Rubin, Zick, 102, 211

sadness, 71, 84–85, 150, 182

Saulny, Susan, 54, 210

Schwartz, Pepper, 104, 109, 112, 211

secure attachment, 2–4, 34, 35, 67, 75

self-evaluation, 125

sensuality, 2–3

separations, **42**–43, 64–65, 69, 78–79, 150–1

sexual desire, 2–3, 5–11, 158, 103–105

sexual dysfunction, 185

sexual obsession, 6

sexual satisfaction, 6–7, **27**, 64, **103**–104

Shaver, Phillip, 2, 34, 208, 209

siblings, **23**, 38, 40, 45, 64, 66–67, **74**–77, 87, 188–9

Silver, Nan, x, 62, 207, 210

single, **23**, 40, **42**–43, 182–183, 202

smoking, **24**, 40, **117**–120

stay-at-home parent, 61–64, 71, **108**–109

stepchildren and stepparents,
30, 43, **44**–47, 164, 188–9,
190–197

Stevenson-Hinde, J., 150, 212

survival, 3, 7, 10, 100, 181,
196–7, 201, 208

tactile stimulation, 2, 33

threats, 76, 98

Toman, Walter, 38, 210

traumatic events, 64, 66, 77, 79,
98, 104, 111, 151

trust, 11, 33–35, 65–69, 106,
204

values, 25, 39, 55, 106–7, 172

Van de Velde, Theo. H., 203,
212

Walant, Karen, 67, 211

Wallerstein, Judith, 36, 65, 72,
209, 210

Williams, Wendy, 106, 211

wisdom, 25, 88

withholding: affection, 77, 82;
finances, 100

Woitiz, Janet, 120, 212

work, **24**, 42, 64, 71, **108**–9, 193

The Prospective
Spouse Checklist

Use a separate list for each member of the couple. Although there is no pass/fail score, more "YES" and fewer "NO" check marks usually point to better odds for marital success.

BASIC INFORMATION	YES	NO
*1. SINGLE		
2. NO CHILDREN		
3. NO PREVIOUS MARRIAGE		
4. SMALL AGE DIFFERENCE		
5. SIMILAR EDUCATION		
6. SIMILAR INTELLIGENCE		
7. SAME RACE, RELIGION AND CULTURE		
8. ADEQUATE OR POTENTIAL ASSETS/INCOME		
FAMILY HISTORY	**YES**	**NO**
*9. WELL TREATED, LOVED AND NURTURED IN EARLY YEARS		
10. SAME CAREGIVER(S) TO AGE THREE		
11. PARENTS REMAINED MARRIED THROUGH TEEN YEARS		
*12. GOOD RELATIONSHIPS WITH PARENTS, SIBLINGS AND GRANDPARENTS		
13. OBSERVED AFFECTION BETWEEN PARENTS		
14. PARENTS: GOOD PHYSICAL/EMOTIONAL HEALTH, NO MAJOR ALCOHOL, DRUG OR OTHER PROBLEMS		
PERSONALITY TRAITS/BEHAVIORS	**YES**	**NO**
15. KIND AND CONSIDERATE		
16. SENSE OF HUMOR		
17. CHEERFUL		
18. HAS FRIENDS		
19. MATURE JUDGMENT		

	YES	NO
20. FLEXIBLE		
21. PROMPT		
22. ORGANIZED AND NEAT		
*23. ABLE TO CONTROL ANGER		
24. WILLING TO ACCEPT ADVICE		
25. GENEROUS		
MUTUAL ELEMENTS OF COMPANIONSHIP	**YES**	**NO**
*26. ENJOY TIME TOGETHER		
*27. SEXUAL ATTRACTION		
*28. AGREEMENT ON MORAL, ETHICAL AND POLITICAL ISSUES		
*29. AGREEMENT ON MAJOR GOALS: HAVING A FAMILY, RELIGIOUS AFFILIATION, CHILDCARE		
30. AGREEMENT ON MONEY MANAGEMENT AND INVESTMENTS		
31. AGREEMENT CONCERNING PETS		
32. ACCEPTANCE OF MATCH BY BOTH FAMILIES		
OTHER PROBLEM AREAS	**YES**	**NO**
*33. NO ADDICTION TO SMOKING, ALCOHOL, DRUGS OR GAMBLING		
*34. NO MAJOR PHYSICAL, MENTAL OR EMOTIONAL HEALTH PROBLEMS		
35. NO MAJOR PAST OR PRESENT LEGAL PROBLEMS		
TOTALS		

We have marked ten of these thirty-five items with asterisks (*).
Think of each as a "RED FLAG" warning and consider each VERY
CAREFULLY. A check mark in the "NO" box for any of these ten
items is serious and should be thoroughly explored.

<u>**notes**</u>

notes

notes

notes

K

CO—O
L_ _